Brochures

that

Work

———————————

David E. Carter
Editor

Suzanna M.W. Brown
Book Designer

Brochures That Work

First published 1998 by Hearst Books International
1350 Avenue of the Americas
New York, NY 10019

ISBN: 0688-16394-7

Distributed in the U.S. and Canada by
Watson-Guptill Publications
1515 Broadway
New York, NY 10036
Tel: (800) 451-1741
            (732) 363-4511 in NJ, AK, HI
Fax: (732) 363-0338

ISBN: 0-8230-6608-8

Distributed throughout the rest of the world by
Hearst Books International
1350 Avenue of the Americas
New York, NY 10019
Fax: (212) 261-6795

First Published in Germany by
Nippan
Nippon Shuppan Hanbai
Deutschland GmbH
Krefelder Str. 85
D-40549 Dusseldorf
Telephone: (0211) 504 8089
Fax: (0211) 504 9326

ISBN: 3-937884-24-4

Printed in Hong Kong by Everbest Printing Company
through Four Colour Imports, Louisville, Kentucky.

When I was asked by my publisher to do a book titled **Brochures that Work**, the main consideration I had was how to present the material in the most useful way.

My first thought was to include snippets from hundreds of brochures, to show a large variety of design styles. But then I realized that would not show the consistency of design throughout a brochure that is so important.

After evaluating several different options, I finally decided to have two pages for each brochure. This way, the cover could be shown, as well as three complete two-page spreads. The resulting layout would let the reader see nearly 100 brochures, and see enough to get a real feel for just what makes the brochure work.

So, here are some outstanding brochures from around the world…brochures that work.

-D. Carter

ARCHITECT

Creative Firm   **Savage Design Group**
Houston, Texas
Client   *FKP Architects*

Cover is line-textured cream stock. First and last pages are lined vellum; first page is printed with logo. Interior is printed on white matte paper. Total measurement is 6" x 9".

VISION **Expert** SOLUTION

"FKP's technical knowledge of the hospital has resulted in a design rich in creativity and very functionally effective."
— Douglas J. Leonard, Chief Operating Officer,
Columbus Regional Hospital, Columbus, Indiana

For FKP healthcare is a specialty. In an industry undergoing quantum shifts in technology, in economics and delivery, we offer objectivity, answers and alternatives.

Our knowledge provides you with direction as you grow and change. Our experience saves you time and money, enabling us to quickly identify core issues and work with skill and flexibility in developing a response.

Focused on the larger picture, we define our priorities as:

+ *Grasping the goals* – through listening

+ *Defining the vision* – through planning

+ *Finding the opportunity* – through analyzing

FKP's focus goes beyond design goals into your business objectives. Often the best answer isn't simply to *build* something – but to change operations, or philosophy, or market position. That's the kind of answer FKP provides.

FOCUS Leader EXPERIENCE

When building is the right answer, FKP will bring your vision to reality. We offer comprehensive services – but what distinguishes FKP is the way our services are provided:

+ *Creatively.* We are setting new standards for innovation in building and operational efficiency.

+ *Adeptly.* Our specialization helps clients stay ahead of trends and industry benchmarks, particularly with delivery of care issues.

+ *Reliably.* Programming, planning, and design are executed through top caliber technical documents that reduce risk and improve control.

FKP brings rigor, discipline and control to the design and delivery process. Confidence comes from our proven ability to balance aesthetic and practical skills.

"Today FKP staff works on-site with the hospital staff to re-create our campus and system to enable us to deliver high quality care in a highly competitive market."
— Phillip Thomas, Vice President,
Presbyterian Hospital of Dallas

RESPONSE Partner SUCCESS

"FKP helped rewrite bylaws, planning guidelines and stage a community conference on healthcare issues as a result of preparing a strategic plan and a master plan to bring unity and direction to our Medical Center."
— Stephen B. Gens, President, Harrington Regional
Medical Center, Amarillo, Texas

You are unique. Your organization is unique. Over the years, FKP has learned to work with the many stakeholders in healthcare and help them find successful solutions:

+ *The Business People.* Who want us to know their business and how to protect their investment.

+ *The Medical People.* Who need us to know their profession and what makes them effective in the work they do.

+ *The Boards and Community People.* Who call for us to know their community and understand their responsibility.

FKP makes no sweeping assumptions and relies on no single formula. Our value lies in knowing how to build the collaboration to support a client's success.

Creative Firm   **Besser Design Group, Inc.**
                Santa Monica, California
Client   *Windstar Cruises*

Binding is glued on this brochure that uses semigloss white papers.
Between front cover and first page is a tear-off postcard. Brochure
measure 7-3/4" x 11".

WIND SPIRIT

7 Day Greek Isles Cruises ~ Wind Spirit
May 16 - October 3, 1998

Day	Ports Of Call	Arrive	Depart
Saturday	Athens, Greece (Piraeus)		5PM
Sunday	Mykonos, Greece	8AM	11PM
Monday	Santorini, Greece	8AM	4PM
Tuesday	Rhodes, Greece	8AM	11PM
Wednesday	Bodrum, Turkey	7AM	6PM
Thursday	Kusadasi, Turkey	8AM	4PM
Friday	At Sea		•
Saturday	Istanbul, Turkey	8AM	•

Length	1998 Sailing Date	Fare
7 Days	May 16, 30	$4,565
7 Days	June 13, 27	$4,565
7 Days	July 11, 25	$4,565
7 Days	August 8, 22	$4,565
7 Days	September 5, 19	$4,565
7 Days	October 3	$4,565

Port charges and taxes of $170 are included in fare shown, but they will not be discounted.

WINDSTAR ADVANCE SAVINGS ADVANTAGE PROGRAM*
Initial ASAP savings of up to $1,319 on the above fares.

7 Day Greek Isles Cruises ~ Wind Spirit
May 23 - October 10, 1998

Day	Ports Of Call	Arrive	Depart
Saturday	Istanbul, Turkey		5PM
Sunday	At Sea		•
Monday	Kusadasi, Turkey	8AM	6PM
Tuesday	Rhodes, Greece	7AM	1PM
Wednesday	Bodrum, Turkey	7AM	5PM
Thursday	Santorini, Greece	11AM	11PM
Friday	Mykonos, Greece	8AM	6PM
Saturday	Athens, Greece (Piraeus)	8AM	•

Length	1998 Sailing Date	Fare
7 Days	May 23	$4,565
7 Days	June 6, 20	$4,565
7 Days	July 4, 18	$4,565
7 Days	August 1, 15, 29	$4,565
7 Days	September 12, 26	$4,565
7 Days	October 10	$4,565

Port charges and taxes of $170 are included in fare shown, but they will not be discounted.

WINDSTAR ADVANCE SAVINGS ADVANTAGE PROGRAM*
Initial ASAP savings of up to $1,319 on the above fares.

WIND STAR

7 Day Greek Isles Cruises ~ Wind Star
May 9 - October 10, 1998

Day	Ports Of Call	Arrive	Depart
Saturday	Athens, Greece (Piraeus)		5PM
Sunday	Mykonos, Greece	8AM	11PM
Monday	Santorini, Greece	8AM	4PM
Tuesday	Rhodes, Greece	8AM	11PM
Wednesday	Bodrum, Turkey	7AM	6PM
Thursday	Kusadasi, Turkey	8AM	4PM
Friday	At Sea		•
Saturday	Istanbul, Turkey	8AM	•

Length	1998 Sailing Date	Fare
7 Days	May 9, 23	$4,565
7 Days	June 6, 20	$4,565
7 Days	July 4, 18	$4,565
7 Days	August 1, 15, 29	$4,565
7 Days	September 5, 19	$4,565
7 Days	October 10	$4,565

Port charges and taxes of $170 are included in fare shown, but they will not be discounted.

WINDSTAR ADVANCE SAVINGS ADVANTAGE PROGRAM*
Initial ASAP savings of up to $1,319 on the above fares.

7 Day Greek Isles Cruises ~ Wind Star
May 16 - October 17, 1998

Day	Ports Of Call	Arrive	Depart
Saturday	Istanbul, Turkey		5PM
Sunday	At Sea		•
Monday	Kusadasi, Turkey	8AM	6PM
Tuesday	Rhodes, Greece	7AM	11PM
Wednesday	Bodrum, Turkey	7AM	5PM
Thursday	Santorini, Greece	11AM	11PM
Friday	Mykonos, Greece	8AM	6PM
Saturday	Athens, Greece (Piraeus)	8AM	•

Length	1998 Sailing Date	Fare
7 Days	May 16, 30	$4,565
7 Days	June 13, 27	$4,565
7 Days	July 11, 25	$4,565
7 Days	August 8, 22	$4,565
7 Days	September 5, 19	$4,565
7 Days	October 3, 17	$4,565

Port charges and taxes of $170 are included in fare shown, but they will not be discounted.

WINDSTAR ADVANCE SAVINGS ADVANTAGE PROGRAM*
Initial ASAP savings of up to $1,319 on the above fares.

*ASAP savings vary by sailing, are available on a first-come, first-served basis and are subject to change without notice.
†Weather permitting.

Rome and the Amalfi Coast

Ooh la la, la dolce vita. Does life get sweeter than sailing the Mediterranean, sprinting with the wind along Europe's most beautiful stretch of coast?

Towering limestone cliffs rise steeply from the sea; lemon groves, vineyards, and pastel villas dot the shore. This is the coastline that's inspired a thousand Ferrari-fueled fantasies; romantic...dramatic...the playground of starlets and kings. You'll feel it as Wind Song glides into Capri next to majestic purring yachts. Or as you sip an espresso in front of the cathedral in Amalfi. Here, as you marvel at the glories of Rome's cathedrals, fountains, bustling piazzas, and stupendous art — here is the pulse of Italian life. One day, it's a jaunt from Livorno to the

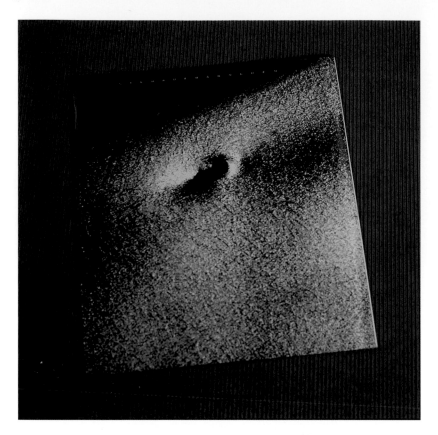

Creative Firm   **House of Design**
                 Graz, Austria
Client   *House of Design*

Brochure measures 8-7/8" x 9-7/8".
It employs perfect binding and is
printed on Phoenix-Imperial white
glossy stock. Both inside covers have
full flaps that fold out.

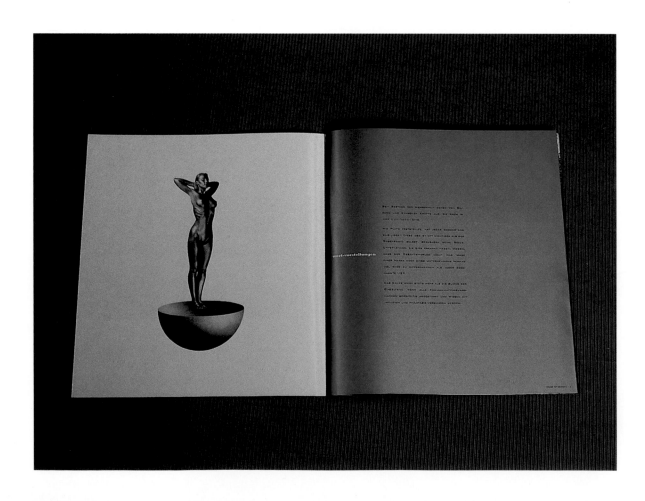

Creative Firm **Clifford Selbert Design**
Inglewood, California
Client *Cal Poly Pomona*

Cover and text pages are printed on corresponding weights of white paper. Outside corners of brochure are rounded. Back inside cover has a flap containing a tear-off response card. Middle spread folds out completely from both sides. Brochure is 6-1/4" x 12".

admissions

"*Cal Poly Pomona is a great value in education. I'd be paying a whole lot more in most other places.*"

DAVIE SILVER MECHANICAL ENGINEERING

Can I afford Cal Poly Pomona?

Our students pay only **10%-15%** of what you'd pay at some other schools.

Am I eligible?
If you're a California resident, a year of a full class load will cost between $1,800 and $1,900, plus books and lab fees—about $500-600. Compare that to similar institutions which can run as high as $10,000 per year for fees alone. If you opt for the convenience of on-campus living, average costs are between $4,000 and $5,500 annually. If you're in the top half of your high school class, you are the kind of person we'd like to meet. We look at your grade point average and scores on pre-admissions tests. If you're from out of state, costs will be somewhat higher. Use the handy postcard in the back of this booklet to request more information.

CAL POLY POMONA *Leading the Next Millennium* **3**

"You just can't find another setting like this in Southern California."

JOY OAKS, LIBERAL STUDIES

What's the campus like?

Beaches, mountains, and deserts are all within 45 minutes' drive from the campus.

Where is it?
In the midst of over 1,400 acres of greenery, you won't believe you're only 32 miles east of downtown Los Angeles. Wooded, rolling hills and pastureland surround a quiet, congenial university campus. Arabian horses graze in our pastures, crops grow in our fields, and the latest technology hums in our classrooms and labs—state-of-the-art in peaceful coexistence with nature. You're centrally located for hundreds of activities such as surfing, snow skiing, desert backpacking and world-famous amusement parks.

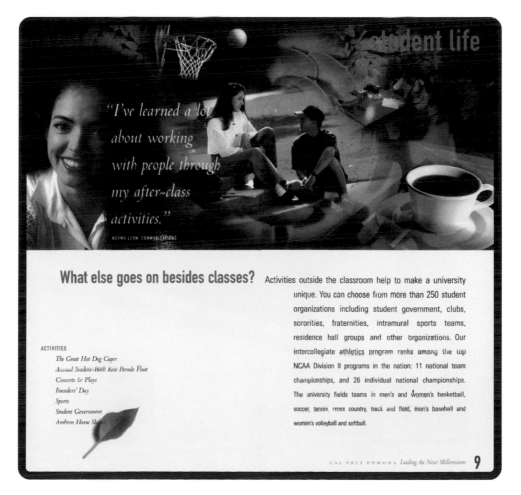

"I've learned a lot about working with people through my after-class activities."

NORMA LEON, COMMUNICATIONS

What else goes on besides classes?

ACTIVITIES
The Great Hot Dog Caper
Annual Student-Built Rose Parade Float
Concerts & Plays
Founders' Day
Sports
Student Government
Arabian Horse Show

Activities outside the classroom help to make a university unique. You can choose from more than 250 student organizations including student government, clubs, sororities, fraternities, intramural sports teams, residence hall groups and other organizations. Our intercollegiate athletics program ranks among the top NCAA Division II programs in the nation: 11 national team championships, and 26 individual national championships. The university fields teams in men's and women's basketball, soccer, tennis, cross country, track and field, men's baseball and women's volleyball and softball.

11

Waterford Harbor

VACATION LIVING EVERY DAY

Creative Firm   **Johnston & Company**
                    Houston, Texas
Client   *Waterford Harbor*

White matte cover is printed with four-color process and lines of varnish. Back inside cover has a pocket which holds more information-specific, smaller, tri-fold brochures. Text pages, 6-1/2" x 10-1/2", are a lighter weight white paper, but also use four-color ink and varnish.

The scenery is at once breathtaking and serene

Within the luxurious gated enclave which is Waterford Harbor, escape is possible at any time of day, every day – whether you feel the softness of an approaching sunset, witness ragingly colored sunrises, experience sparkling mid-day views or sail in darkness across the waters that surround us.

Those who live here savor all the moments, and view their lifestyle as an extended vacation might be experienced on some distant shore. Yet, here, the shore is at your back door. For, in Waterford Harbor home sites are at water's edge or within a pebble's throw where the Gulf Coast's natural wonders unfold and take solid hold of mind and spirit.

Homesites are situated 14 feet above sea level, providing a base measure of weather security as well as aesthetics.

24-hour manned security gates contribute to resident peace-of-mind.

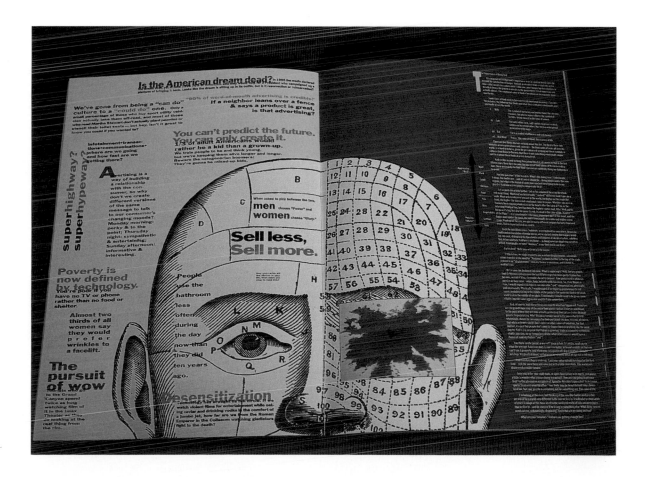

Creative Firm   **Rousso + Associates**
                 Atlanta, Georgia
Client   *Rousso + Associates*

Spiral-bound brochure arrives in a printed brown cardboard box. Several colors of metallic ink and silver foil stamping adorn the black cover. Fibered ecru paper alternates with slick, glossy white paper for the text pages. Brochure measure 9" x 7".

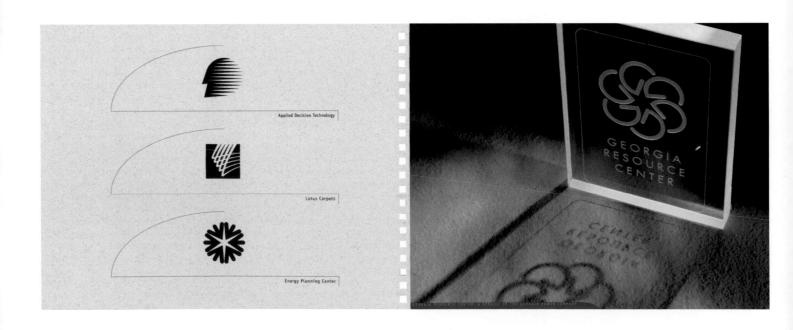

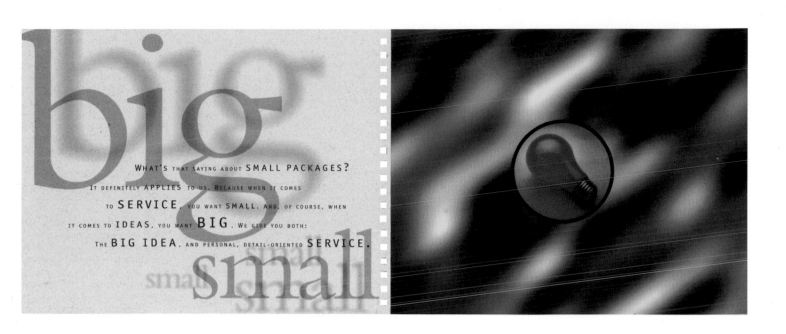

WHAT'S THAT SAYING ABOUT SMALL PACKAGES?
IT DEFINITELY APPLIES TO US. BECAUSE WHEN IT COMES
TO SERVICE, YOU WANT SMALL. AND, OF COURSE, WHEN
IT COMES TO IDEAS, YOU WANT BIG. WE GIVE YOU BOTH:
THE BIG IDEA, AND PERSONAL, DETAIL-ORIENTED SERVICE.

Services

It's As Easy As

CALL FORWARDING

Keep In Touch

Creative Firm   **B•Bi Studio Inc.**
                Tokyo, Japan
Client   *Hikomizuno College of Jewelry*

Tall brochure measures 5" x 14-1/4". Off-white, dull stock of the same weight is used for both cover and inside of brochure.

WATCH MAKER 1

ウォッチメーカー初級コース

一流のウォッチメーカーは、1000分の5ミリの違いがわかります。

それを目指すために、感覚を回復し、

工具を作り直しします(新品の工具は、そのままでは使えません)。

工具を見れば、その人の腕がわかると言われるほど大切なことです。

この6ヵ月で、シンプルな機械式時計の分解、洗浄、組立、

注油を中心に実習します。歴史、構造等や毎日の講義は、視聴覚機器を

使ってわかりやすく行います。設備機器も、(社)日本時計輸入協会の協力で

スイス製(ベルジョン)を中心にプロ仕様のものがそろいましたので、

プロの仕事場として充分な環境です。

初級だけでは、ほんの入り口、中級に進んだ時

初めてプロへの道が開け、時計のおもしろさがわかってきます。

営業・販売のための基本技術講座

営業・販売の方が知っておきたい時計技術の知識を、初級の学科授業を

公開して8回で行います。新入社員教育にご利用下さい。

設備機器は、プロが使う
スイス製(ベルジョン)のものです。

基礎ムーブメント(機械式)

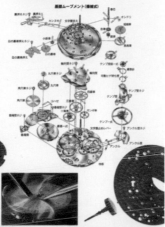

初 級 6ヶ月40回100時間	

※初の学科が、営業・販売のための基本講座に公開されている授業です。

視聴覚機器をフルに使って、
わかりやすく行います。

WATCH MAKER 2

ウォッチメーカー中級コース

初級を修了した人が進級するコース。ここからが本番です。

ここからは、自動巻きムーブメントを使って、

本格的な調整を実習します。時計の心臓部である脱進機やテン真、

ヒゲの調整は緊張感いっぱいです。

ここでは、様々なコンプリケーションウォッチ(複雑多機能時計)の

構造も学びます。これで卒業ですが、就職してからも

一流を目指して腕を磨いていきます。

中 級 6ヶ月36回90時間	

ウォッチメーカーコース入学要項	
期間・曜日 時間予定	初級コース 週2回 4〜9月の6ヵ月 火・木 18:00〜20:30(予定) 営業・販売のための基本技術講座 週1回 4月より6回 火 18:00〜20:30(予定) 中級コース 週2回 10〜3月の6ヵ月 火・木 18:00〜20:30(予定)

学 費

このコースの学費納入には、JCB、VISA、NICOSカードが利用できます。時期によってはボーナス一括払いが、又一括払いが困難な方はNICOSカードを利用して6回まで月賦払いで受講できます。

初級コース	入学金 40,000円 授業料 149,900円 施設料 40,000円 合計 229,900円 教材費 80,000円の予定(スイス製リストウォッチ含)
中級コース	授業料 149,900円 施設料 40,000円 合計 189,900円 教材費 30,000円の予定
営業・販売のための基本技術講座	願書登録料 8,000円 授業料 29,000円 施設料 8,000円 合計 45,000円 教材費 5,000円

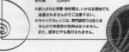

Creative Firm   **Allan Burrows Limited**
Ingatestone, England
Client   *Ford Motor Company Limited*

This brochure really has two covers. Outside cover is embossed tan stock, and has fold-out inside flaps. Inside cover is printed on matte white, card stock. Inside pages are matte white, text weight. One page of brochure repeats cover fold out, offering information charts.

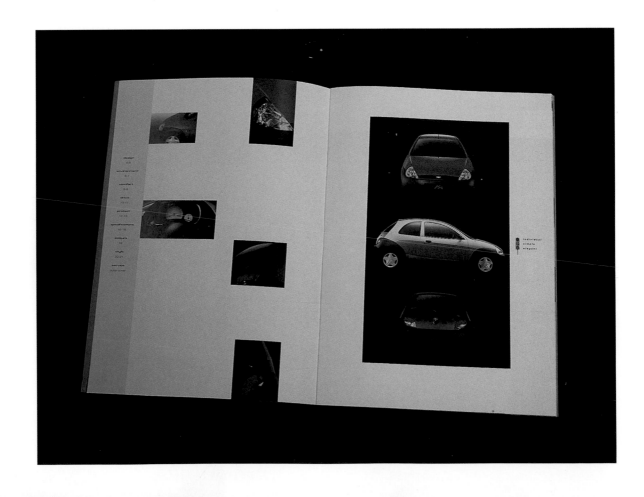

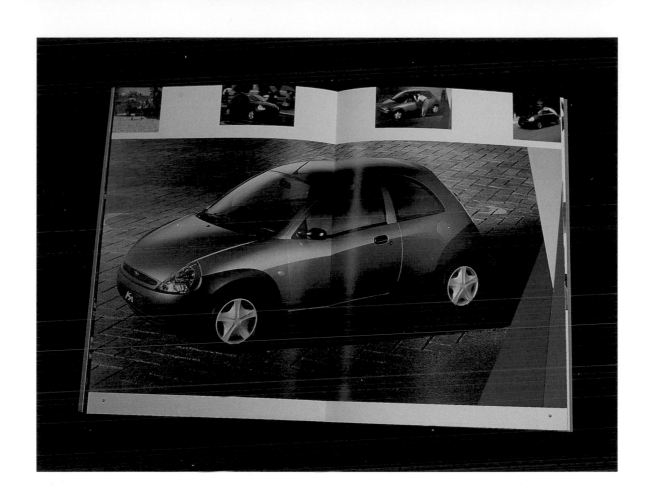

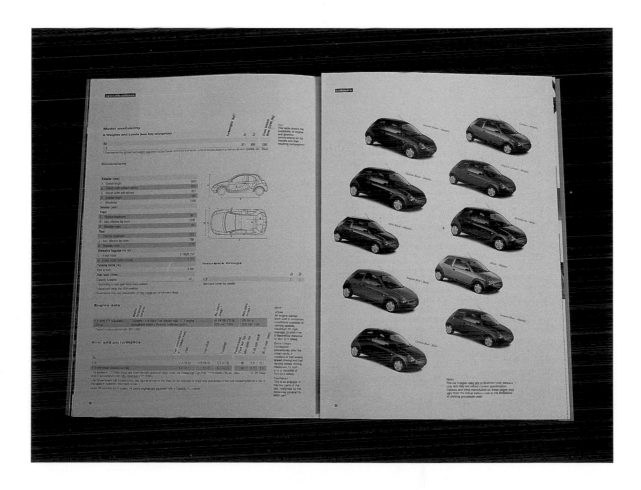

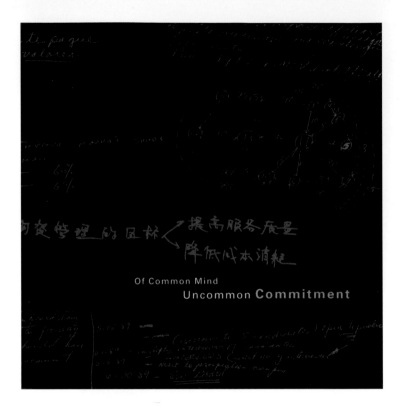

Of Common Mind
Uncommon **Commitment**

Creative Firm   **Simantel Group**
  Peoria, Illinois
Client   *Caterpillar Inc.*

Both cover and text pages are white matte stock, the cover being heavier than the interior of this 9-1/2" square brochure.

Employee Education

At Caterpillar, we believe in the personal growth, capability and advancement of our employees. That's why, since Day One, we've made a large investment in their education. Every year, hundreds of Cat employees continue their education and earn degrees. And every day, thousands of employees participate in seminars and training sessions worldwide. Employee education plays a big role in the character of Caterpillar. Just ask Pam Rothbart, Truck Engine District Manager.

When I started as a machinist apprentice at Caterpillar, I had completed about two and a half years of college. Thanks to the Caterpillar Educational Assistance Program, I not only finished my college degree, but also began work on my MBA.

That's when the economic downturn hit. People around me got their layoff notices, but my college degree saved me. I was transferred to the Marketing Training Program, where I continued my education, and eventually earned my MBA.

At the time I began finishing my BA, I was working full time and going to school nights and weekends. It was tough. If Caterpillar hadn't paid for 100% of my education, I could never have afforded to go back to college.

As far as the quality of work and job enrichment, education has made a huge difference in my life.

I have the self-confidence because I have the education. I believe in it so strongly, I pass on the gift of education that Caterpillar gave to me through college scholarships.

Pam's story is one which is true for a vast number of employees who have benefited from the Caterpillar Educational Assistance Program throughout our history. Education has increased our employees' abilities and their self-confidence. It has given them a brighter future. And when our employees are stronger, they're able to contribute more to the company, making Caterpillar stronger.

Education was the key to a different life.

Pam Rothbart

1925

Apprenticeships:
1925 – ongoing: Considered by many to be the "backbone" of Caterpillar, this invaluable four-year program was designed to provide young talent with solid training and a working knowledge of the manufacturing process. This program produced many top administrators including several Cat VP's, a president and a chairman.

Technical Skills Training:
1925 – ongoing: Designed to upgrade the skills of our manufacturing employees, this program provides technical training for such job-related skills as math and blueprint reading. This training is free of charge for participants who attend classes either on or off shift.

Mentoring Programs:
1925 – ongoing: Mentoring is an important aspect of personal development. Many Caterpillar employees volunteer time to act as role models in a number of different environments for youth and adults alike.

Caterpillar Training Institute:
1925 – ongoing: The Caterpillar Training Institute offers education and training services to worldwide employees, dealers, suppliers, and other related organizations at Caterpillar. A wide range of training topics include: business management, manufacturing, office support, quality, sales and technical training.

Two-year Training for Employees:
1930's – 1980's: This program was introduced to allow seasoned factory employees the opportunity to upgrade into skilled labor positions by participating in a two-year apprentice-type program. This produced highly skilled workers in such areas as machining, welding and sheet metal.

1930

School-to-Work Concept Programs:
1930's – ongoing: Recognizing the importance of an effective school-to-work transition; Caterpillar is a leader in school-to-work programs such as high school and college co-op programs and internships. Hundreds of individuals each year are given this transition experience at Caterpillar facilities worldwide.

College Graduate Recruiting:
1931 – ongoing: To build a better work force, Caterpillar conducts worldwide searches for the most talented graduates from the best engineering and business schools.

Advanced Management Programs:
1940's – ongoing: Originally designed to help groom and prepare experienced managers for increased global responsibilities, this program is taught by executive-level Cat administrators as well as professors from universities around the world.

Junior Achievement:
1946 – ongoing: Through the efforts of former Caterpillar Chairman, Louis B. Neumiller, Junior Achievement was introduced to the Caterpillar family. This national program allows high school students to experience all facets of business management. Caterpillar was awarded the first Spirit of Free Enterprise Award in 1995.

Supervisor Selection & Training Program:
1950's – ongoing: This program provides factory and office employees an opportunity to receive training necessary to qualify for management positions. It also aids transition into new management roles.

Dealer Education

As evidence of our commitment to our dealers, Caterpillar has created a division dedicated solely to dealer support and education. Thousands of Cat dealers participate in our seminars and education every year. At this very moment, field engineers around the world are involved in training. We've learned these educational efforts are making a difference in the lives and careers of dealers' employees like Phil Colman, Regional Product Support Manager of H. Leverton Limited, U.K.

As a teenager, I loved to tinker with my motorbike. Somehow I was lucky enough to land an apprenticeship as a mechanic. I went to night school for my mechanic qualifications, while I spent five days a week in the workshop. At the same time, I was also attending college to become an engineer.

I grabbed an opportunity with Zahid Tractor (a Caterpillar dealership) to go to the Middle East. Then I was hired by H. Leverton Ltd. and moved up from workshop engineer to field service engineer to service supervisor in just three years. And Caterpillar training played a key role in almost every step of my advancement. Once you've shown willingness and aptitude, you can get on a fast track.

I was always afraid of public speaking…I guess most people are. In a recent survey, respondents listed their top two fears as public speaking, followed by nuclear war. Isn't that something? So I enrolled in a communication skills course, which helped me a lot. It's all a confidence thing.

The commitment Caterpillar has to its dealers translates into hundreds of educational opportunities — opportunities which can spell success for our dealers in a variety of ways. Although the cost of developing these materials and seminars is overwhelming, the results are even more overwhelming. Our education and training efforts help ensure Cat dealers remain the best dealer network in the industry.

Without the training, I don't think I would have been considered at all for some of the more senior positions.

Phil Colman

1950					**1968**					

Educational Assistance Program: 1950's – ongoing: Learning is a way of life for Caterpillar employees. If academic requirements are met, Caterpillar provides reimbursement of 100% of tuition, registration, and lab fees for employees desiring to pursue their college education.

Caterpillar Foundation: 1952 – ongoing: Each year Caterpillar donates millions of dollars to support education in the form of scholarships, grants, materials and manpower.

College Graduate Training Program: 1960 – ongoing: To produce highly skilled supervisors, this program gives recent graduates the necessary training and management skills in all areas of the company from engineering to accounting.

European Dealer Service Training: 1961 – ongoing: Caterpillar enjoys a reputation for excellence in worldwide service. Taught in six languages, this dealer training program focuses on service-related topics and new product developments. Six Training Centers are located in Tokyo, Japan; Singapore; Melbourne, Australia; Beijing, China; Malaga, Spain; and São Paulo, Brazil.

Global Service Training: 1961 – ongoing: Designed to reach the most remote international regions, traveling workshops are conducted throughout the world. Training programs, with curriculum determined by regional needs, are conducted in Beirut, Lebanon; Lagos, Nigeria; and Johannesburg, South Africa.

Disadvantaged Youth Program: 1968 – 1972: Designed to help disadvantaged high school students, this program taught basic secretarial and clerical skills on the job. Many of the participants went on to graduate and work at Caterpillar.

Degree Option Program: 1970's – ongoing: Created to bridge the commercialization gap between engineering and manufacturing personnel. Students graduating from this workplace training program receive a BS in Manufacturing Engineering Technology.

Skills Inventory Systems: 1970's – ongoing: Caterpillar pioneered the idea of a company-wide database of employee training skills and education levels. This helps our employees identify skills needed for future promotions and job opportunities.

Tomorrow's Scientists, Technicians and Managers: 1970's – ongoing: Caterpillar led the way in the development of these programs which help increase minority students' interest in science and technical fields.

Vocational Industrial Clubs of America (VICA): 1970's – ongoing: Our belief in a brighter future in education for today's youth is evident in our ongoing support of VICA, a leading vocational-technical educational organization. In fact, VICA's annual corporate support award, the Pat Dalton Award, is named for and given in memory of a former Caterpillar manager.

Community Outreach Education

Not only does Caterpillar allow release-time for our dedicated people to assist educational organizations, we donate millions of dollars to schools throughout the world. In every community where we live and work, we support education. Caterpillar people serve on school boards and as teachers. We award scholarships and offer work-study programs. We raise hopes and expectations. For example, there's the uplifting story of Jerry Johnson, New Product Introduction Manager.

When I was asked to volunteer my time as Board Chairman to help build the first permanent campus of a local community college, I was honored. And Caterpillar wholeheartedly supported me.

So during Caterpillar company time, I helped to fund and build the community college. I'm proud to know that many residents who never could have attended college otherwise, are now able to. Especially disadvantaged students.

Thousands of Caterpillar employees just like me give of their time and talents to help out in their communities. Cat has been very gracious and loyal to those employees, giving them time away from work for educational reasons.

Caterpillar not only supported my community college project by giving me the time off, but also gave a generous contribution. The company even donated material and other equipment to the School of Welding. Caterpillar is absolutely committed to education.

At Caterpillar, we believe in education for everyone. Throughout our history, we've helped provide opportunities for our neighbors worldwide. Tens of thousands of people around the globe have benefited from Caterpillar's continuing commitment to education. You see, at Caterpillar, we believe that living truly is learning.

Caterpillar makes a significant contribution to education that no one sees.

P.S. Jerry Johnson

1970						**1992**					

Caterpillar Overseas, SA Dealer Management Simulation: 1970's – ongoing: This business learning tool simulates actual dealer marketing challenges and practices in the current worldwide marketplace.

Caterpillar Matching Funds: 1979 – ongoing: Our commitment to education is again revealed by this program in which Caterpillar matches employee donations to colleges, universities and the arts.

Dealer Apprenticeships: 1980's – ongoing: This two-year cooperative program brings together Cat dealers and technical universities to generate qualified technicians to service Cat equipment on all seven continents.

Faculty Internships: 1980 – ongoing: This program allows university professors to share their academic knowledge of manufacturing while receiving real-world, hands-on industrial experience.

Factory Engineering Education Program: 1986 – ongoing: A joint effort between Caterpillar and innovative community colleges. This unique associate degree program is designed to upgrade the educational level of factory engineering personnel and to keep employees current with new technologies.

High School Academies: 1990 – ongoing: Caterpillar supports and helps develop high school academies worldwide.

World in Motion: 1992 – ongoing: Created by the Society of Automotive Engineers (SAE), this program provides supplemental ideas to traditional physical science curriculum grade schools throughout the U.S. and Canada. Caterpillar engineers volunteer to implement this creative, hands-on educational experience.

New Generation: 1994 – ongoing: Created in the Commonwealth of Independent States, this program affords mining students the opportunity to study the world of mining and mining equipment in the United States.

Work Force Preparation Initiative Program: 1994 – ongoing: A joint effort between Caterpillar, Cat dealers and suppliers, and community colleges, this one-of-a-kind program gives high school students firsthand experience allowing them to work with machine operators and assemblers.

Big Iron University: 1995 – ongoing: This worldwide dealer education program is presented by the Caterpillar Mining Group. To stay abreast of the newest mining technologies, Cat dealer salespeople learn the latest advancements in the mining industry.

China Human Resource Exchange: 1995 – ongoing: This three-year program brings human resource managers of China's largest companies to the U.S. to exchange information related to HR policies. Likewise, U.S. managers meet in China to gain "cross-cultural" information on Chinese HR policies.

RETIREMENT PLANNING GUIDE

Developed by Washington Mutual and its affiliate, Murphey Favre, Inc., which offer
Composite Group of Mutual Funds and WM Life Insurance Company Annuities.

Creative Firm   **Phinney/Bischoff Design House**
                 Seattle, Washington
Client   *Washington Mutual*

Both cover and text pages, though different weights, are printed on white matte papers. Back cover has an inside pocket in which staggered, information-specific pages are inserted. Outside measurement is 9" x 12" with the inside pages slightly narrower.

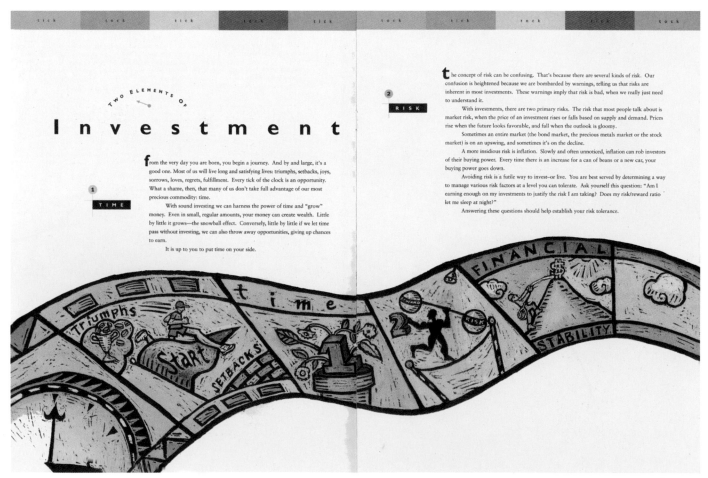

TWO ELEMENTS OF

Investment

1 TIME

from the very day you are born, you begin a journey. And by and large, it's a good one. Most of us will live long and satisfying lives: triumphs, setbacks, joys, sorrows, loves, regrets, fulfillment. Every tick of the clock is an opportunity. What a shame, then, that many of us don't take full advantage of our most precious commodity: time.

With sound investing we can harness the power of time and "grow" money. Even in small, regular amounts, your money can create wealth. Little by little it grows—the snowball effect. Conversely, little by little if we let time pass without investing, we can also throw away opportunities, giving up chances to earn.

It is up to you to put time on your side.

2 RISK

the concept of risk can be confusing. That's because there are several kinds of risk. Our confusion is heightened because we are bombarded by warnings, telling us that risks are inherent in most investments. These warnings imply that risk is bad, when we really just need to understand it.

With investments, there are two primary risks. The risk that most people talk about is market risk, when the price of an investment rises or falls based on supply and demand. Prices rise when the future looks favorable, and fall when the outlook is gloomy.

Sometimes an entire market (the bond market, the precious metals market or the stock market) is on an upswing, and sometimes it's on the decline.

A more insidious risk is inflation. Slowly and often unnoticed, inflation can rob investors of their buying power. Every time there is an increase for a can of beans or a new car, your buying power goes down.

Avoiding risk is a futile way to invest—or live. You are best served by determining a way to manage various risk factors at a level you can tolerate. Ask yourself this question: "Am I earning enough on my investments to justify the risk I am taking? Does my risk/reward ratio let me sleep at night?"

Answering these questions should help establish your risk tolerance.

Imagine your retirement: **AGE 23**

many young adults find it difficult to start saving and investing money. Some are just out of school and working and earning for the first time. The disposable income is often a siren call: Spend! Consume! Others acknowledge the worth of investing, but feel they must put off the decision until later.

But the fact is, if these new wage-earning consumers begin saving just a small amount every month, two important things will happen to them—good things.

First, if a young woman or man at age 23 can save and invest $100 a month for just five years, he or she will have earned a small fortune by the retirement time of 68: that is the power—some say the "miracle"— of compounding. Put another way, by skipping pizza and a movie ($15 tax and tip included) twice a week, and regularly investing that cash, he or she will have earned more than $105,000 on a total investment of $6,000, assuming a modest 7% rate of return.

More importantly, he or she will have developed a saving and investing habit—one that should provide financial health for a lifetime.

Still, it isn't always easy to make the investment. A young couple with a baby, for example, may feel they don't have money in the budget to invest: their money, for the short term, is invested in formula and diaper service. But once that phase has ended, the couple can cancel the service and—instead of expanding their budget—begin investing, say, $50 a month. Once it becomes a routine, you will be amazed at how rapidly your wealth will grow.

"i don't know where all this money goes, but it sure goes fast!"

If young adults think they have tight budgets, families with children feel as if they've opened the door and watched all their hard-earned money fly out.

The financial demands of the mid-30s family seem never-ending: your kids need clothes, you need two cars (one bigger than you'd ever imagined owning), the food budget is huge, the eight-year-old needs braces and you're thinking about an addition on the house. Or perhaps your parents need medical and financial assistance. In any case, at this time in life you're likely to feel financially swamped.

Imagine your retirement: **AGE 38**

It is very easy at this point to compromise your savings habit to finance your monthly bills. Our advice: your savings IS a monthly bill—and very possibly the most important one you have. Don't break the savings habits you have made.

If you are going to break a habit, choose one less critical to your retirement security. Buy the cheap ice cream instead of premium, and wear Polyblend instead of wool; juggle the bills and get the washer repaired instead of buying a new one. Because the awful truth is, you cannot buy back any of those years in which you DIDN'T invest. That, unfortunately, is the flip side of the miracle of compounding. But you still have some time left.

---

the late 40s and early 50s can be a very satisfying time of life. The children have moved away, but not too far. Many people are at the peak of their professional or business form, but not over the hill.

Financially, you may be making very good money. Since your expenses are smaller, you're probably keeping most of what you earn. you're not buying any more houses or boats or additions to the house. In fact, you might sell the big house and buy a smaller one.

Imagine your retirement: **AGE 55**

In short, you likely have the highest earnings and the highest discretionary income of any period in your life.

This is also the period when it is most important to put as much money as you can into your own personal retirement plans. You may have two or three IRAs from the 1980s, and you're probably in some sort of employer-sponsored retirement plan. You may also have other investments scattered, including mint proof silver dollars you accumulated when you were in high school.

It's time to make two vital calculations: how much current income you can put into your retirement fund every month, and how much money you will need at retirement. Both results are probably more than you would have imagined.

Many people make a guess, and then hope. That's usually not good enough. If you're financially savvy, sit down for a couple of hours: add up what your needs will be, and determine how much you'll have by age 65 or so. If you're not a financial wiz, don't be shy about finding one you can trust—Washington Mutual can help.

This is your future, remember.

Either way, this is a critical time—and a wonderful opportunity to get a better idea of what your retirement will be like.

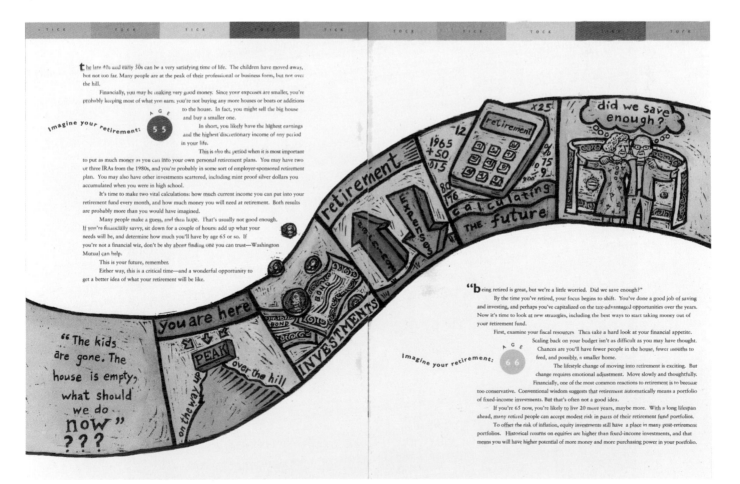

"being retired is great, but we're a little worried. Did we save enough?"

By the time you've retired, your focus begins to shift. You've done a good job of saving and investing, and perhaps you've capitalized on the tax-advantaged opportunities over the years. Now it's time to look at new strategies, including the best ways to start taking money out of your retirement fund.

First, examine your fiscal resources. Then take a hard look at your financial appetite. Scaling back on your budget isn't as difficult as you may have thought. Chances are you'll have fewer people in the house, fewer mouths to feed, and possibly, a smaller home.

Imagine your retirement: **AGE 66**

The lifestyle change of moving into retirement is exciting. But change requires emotional adjustment. Move slowly and thoughtfully.

Financially, one of the most common reactions to retirement is to become too conservative. Conventional wisdom suggests that retirement automatically means a portfolio of fixed-income investments. But that's often not a good idea.

If you're 65 now, you're likely to live 20 more years, maybe more. With a long lifespan ahead, many retired people can accept modest risk in parts of their retirement fund portfolios.

To offset the risk of inflation, equity investments still have a place in many post-retirement portfolios. Historical returns on equities are higher than fixed-income investments, and that means you will have higher potential of more money and more purchasing power in your portfolio.

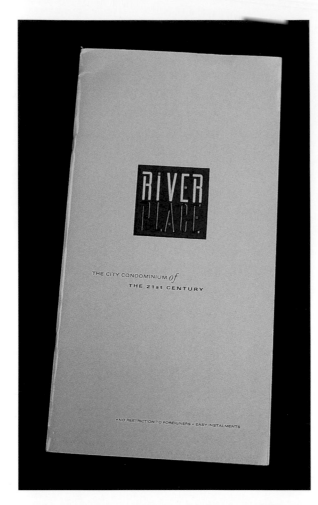

Creative Firm   **KINGGRAPHIC**
Hong Kong, China
Client   *Far East Organization*

Tall brochure (8" x 15-5/8") has die-cut,
varnished, white glossy cover with fold-out
inside flaps. Cover also uses embossing in
logo area and silver foil stamping. Square die
cut, fold outs, foil stamping, and varnished
printing are mimicked inside.

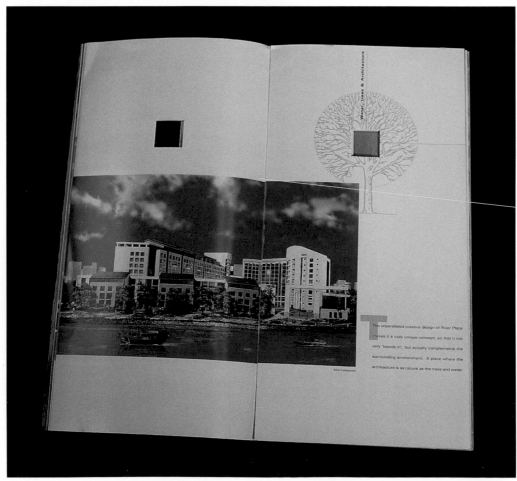

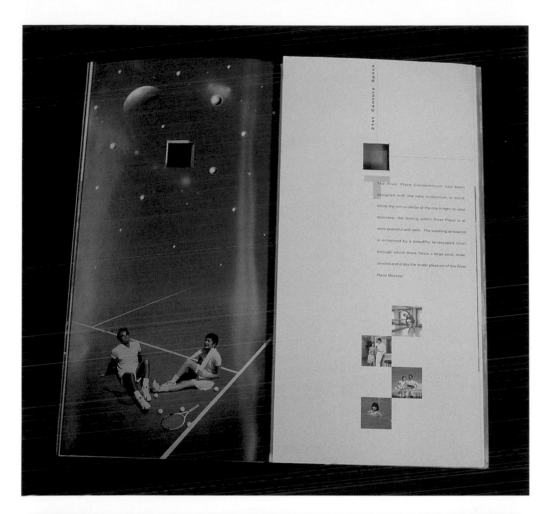

The River Place Condominium has been designed with the new millennium in mind. While the convenience of the city is right on your doorstep, the feeling within River Place is at once peaceful and calm. The soothing ambience is enhanced by a beautiful landscaped court through which there flows a large pool; relax, unwind and enjoy the sheer pleasure of the River Place lifestyle.

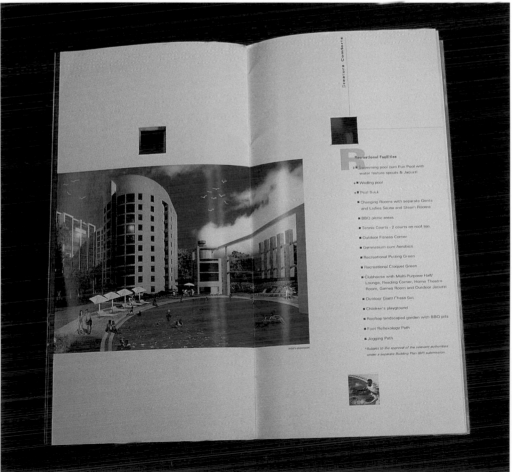

Recreational Facilities

■ Swimming pool cum Fun Pool with water feature spouts & Jacuzzi
■ Wading pool
■ Pool Deck
■ Changing Rooms with separate Gents and Ladies Sauna and Steam Rooms
■ BBQ picnic areas
■ Tennis Courts - 2 courts on roof top
■ Outdoor Fitness Corner
■ Gymnasium cum Aerobics
■ Recreational Putting Green
■ Recreational Croquet Green
■ Clubhouse with Multi-Purpose Hall/ Lounge, Reading Corner, Home Theatre Room, Games Room and Outdoor Jacuzzi
■ Outdoor Giant Chess Set
■ Children's playground
■ Rooftop landscaped garden with BBQ pits
■ Foot Reflexology Path
■ Jogging Path

Subject to the approval of the relevant authorities under a separate Building Plan (BP) submission.

Artist's impression

Creative Firm   **Savage Design Group, Inc.**
                    Houston, Texas
Client   *Coastal Securities*

Maroon cover boasts thermography and
circular die cut. Edge of circle is blind
embossed. At 4-1/16" x 9"', cover is
slightly wider than inside pages and is of a
subtly textured stock. Text pages are
printed on white matte paper. First page is
a full foldout.

NAVIGATING THE CHALLENGES
OF A TURBULENT MARKETPLACE

*Managing the ebb and flow of today's market
influences is more difficult than ever before.
Skill and experience are no longer the only
determining factors. Success demands information, huge amounts of it. More important*

*than the raw data, however, is the power to
view it from many distinct vantage points.
Changing your perspective and your approach
to trading is of paramount importance in
protecting your assets and creating new
opportunities as we look to the future.*

The myriad of activities in America's trillion-dollar fixed income marketplace constitutes an arena of constant opportunity. At Coastal Securities, uncovering and exploiting that opportunity for institutional

investors is the cornerstone of our business. Our combination of specialized market knowledge, securities inventories and integrated analytical tools enables us to provide you with timely market advice, prompt executions and a unique measure of personal attentiveness.

A Myriad of Services

As a registered dealer in government, agency, corporate and mortgage-backed instruments, Coastal Securities provides clients a complete range of fixed income services, in addition to making markets in municipal bonds and OTC equities. We also offer comprehensive portfolio analysis and cash management services, and act as a financial advisor for various municipalities.

Our Distinguished Past

An uncompromising dedication to consistent performance, regardless of marketplace conditions, has allowed us to provide superior investment and finance services. As we have grown and prospered, our professionals have built a distinguished history of counsel to clients in the Southwest and across the nation.

Unparalleled Expertise and Efficiency

Our traders, salespeople, investment bankers and support personnel work together as a single unit to bring you more than combined experience. The benefits of our cohesive organization are realized in a number of ways:

- Decisive reactions to market changes
- Effective access to capital markets
- Extra measure of personal attentiveness

A Bright Future

Today, our people and technology stand ready to serve in more powerful ways than ever before, providing a combination of insight and foresight intended to help you make decisions faster and better than ever before.

Comprehensive Portfolio Database

CoastalView operates atop an integrated database that provides access to critical sources of information pertinent to the fixed income marketplace. The data is continually and automatically updated. So you have immediate access to the following information and much more:

General Marketplace Information

- Government Agency Bonds
- Corporate Bonds
- Mortgage-Backed Bonds

Individual Portfolio Information

- Current Portfolio Documentation
- Historical Portfolio Documentation
- Periodic Portfolio Reporting

Powerful Bond Analytics

Powerful new analytical applications have been built into CoastalView to help provide information and answers for a number of inquiries in a matter of moments.

- CMO Cashflows
- Total Returns
- Prices
- Yields

View Alternative Portfolio Structures

With CoastalView, you can rely less on intuition and more on answers. You now have the tools and data necessary to analyze the effects of potential changes in your portfolio and in the marketplace.

- Evaluate multiple position alternatives
- See how your portfolio will react to changes in the marketplace
- Restructure your entire portfolio

Coastal Securities presents an innovative resource for managing your fixed income investments–CoastalView. It's a powerful new tool and a bold new way of looking at your portfolio. This complete portfolio-based

approach to trading provides many new perspectives on the marketplace. Perspectives that help you illuminate obstacles and opportunities. With CoastalView, you stand better prepared than ever before to navigate the market's advances and declines.

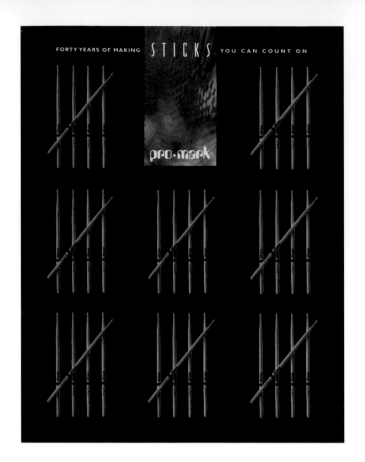

Creative Firm **Steve Sessions, Inc.**
Houston, Texas
Client *Promark*

Four-color process printing is employed throughout entire brochure. Cover and inside pages are the same text weight paper. Brochure measure 8-1/2" x 11".

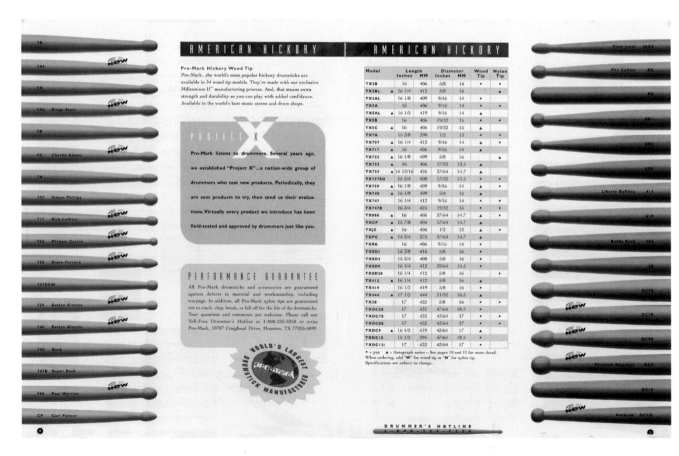

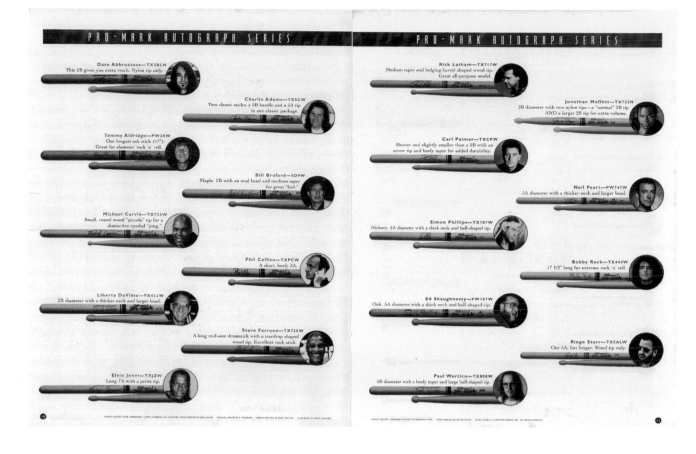

Dave Abbruzzese—TX2BLN
This 2B gives you extra reach. Nylon tip only.

Charlie Adams—TX5CW
Two classic sticks; a 5B handle and a 5A tip in one classic package.

Tommy Aldridge—PW2SW
Our longest oak stick (17").
Great for slammin' rock 'n' roll.

Bill Bruford—SD9W
Maple. 2B with an oval bead and medium taper for great "feel."

Michael Carvin—TX733W
Small, round wood "piccolo" tip for a distinctive cymbal "ping."

Phil Collins—TXPCW
A short, beefy 3A.

Liberty DeVitto—TX412W
2B diameter with a thicker neck and larger bead.

Steve Ferrone—TX735W
A long mid-size drumstick with a teardrop shaped wood tip. Excellent rock stick.

Elvin Jones—TXJZW
Long 7A with a petite tip.

Rick Latham—TX717W
Medium taper and bulging-barrel shaped wood tip. Great all-purpose model.

Jonathan Moffett—TX722N
2B diameter with two nylon tips—a "normal" 2B tip AND a larger 2S tip for extra volume.

Carl Palmer—TXCPW
Shorter and slightly smaller than a 5B with an arrow tip and beefy taper for added durability.

Neil Peart—PW747W
5A diameter with a thicker neck and larger bead.

Simon Phillips—TX707W
Hickory. 5A diameter with a thick neck and ball-shaped tip.

Bobby Rock—TX444W
17 1/2" long for extreme rock 'n' roll.

Ed Shaughnessy—PW707W
Oak. 5A diameter with a thick neck and ball-shaped tip.

Ringo Starr—TX5ALW
Our 5A, but longer. Wood tip only.

Paul Wertico—TX808W
5B diameter with a beefy taper and large ball-shaped tip.

Professional quality keyboard mallets at an affordable price. Polished birch handles are guaranteed not to warp. Generally, the softer the mallet head, the "darker" or "warmer" the tone. Experiment with different mallets to discover your sound. For example, cord mallets used on marimba provide a brighter sound and quicker response than yarn. Yarn mallets used on vibes mean a warmer sound. Pro-Mark mallets are ideal for students and professionals alike. Remember, our reputation is in your hands. Sold in pairs.

Keyboard Percussion Mallets

Model	Description	Suggested Use
PK71	Soft Yarn	Marimba
PK73	Medium Yarn	Marimba
PK75	Hard Yarn	Marimba
PK91	Soft Cord	Vibes
PK93	Medium Cord	Vibes
PK95	Hard Cord	Vibes
PK21	Soft Rubber	Full Range Marimba
PK23	Medium Rubber	Full Range Marimba
PK25	Hard Rubber	Marimba/Xylophone
PK61	Phenolic	Xylophone/Bells
PK62	Brass	Bells

Drum Corps Marching Mallets

High quality, affordable marching mallets are perfect for limited budgets. Solid felt heads epoxied to lightweight, black satin aluminum shafts. Soft, non-slip grips. Bell Lyra mallets feature acrylic or brass heads on sturdy poly handles. March with Pro-Mark, and you'll march with confidence. Sold in pairs.

Marching Mallets

Model	Mallet Type	Head Size Inches	Length Inches
M322L	Bass Drum	2 1/2 Felt	14 1/8
M321M	Bass Drum	2 Felt	14 1/8
M320S	Bass Drum	1 3/4 Felt	14 1/8
M330T	Multi-tenor	1 5/16 Felt	14 3/8
M331T	Multi-tenor	1 1/8 Acrylic	14 3/8
M332T	Multi-tenor	13/16 Acrylic	14 3/8
M340B	Bell Lyra	1 Acrylic	15 3/8
M341B	Bell Lyra	3/4 Brass	15 1/8

Specifications are subject to change.

EVELYN GLENNIE MODELS

EVELYN GLENNIE, O.B.E. Grammy Award-winning Evelyn Glennie is an internationally known and respected solo percussionist. In addition, she has performed with most of the world's major symphony orchestras. An accomplished composer, Ms. Glennie also writes for television and motion pictures. She is the recipient of numerous accolades including the Royal Philharmonic Society's "Soloist Of The Year" award. She was named an Officer of the British Empire (O.B.E.) in 1993.

Snare Drumsticks
These American Hickory drumsticks are designed for multiple percussion uses. The 739 is a 5A diameter for delicate passages, while the 740 is a 2B diameter for producing more volume. Both are 16 1/8" long and feature the same size wood tip...barrel-shaped for maximum articulation.

Marimba/Vibe Mallets
Designed by Ms. Glennie, these extra-dense heads accentuate the true fundamental tone of mallet instruments without sacrificing those desirable overtones. Slightly heavier heads mean more sound with less effort. Polished birch handles. 16 3/8" long. Sold in pairs. Three hardnesses. EG1--Soft, EG3--Medium, EG5--Hard

ROBERT VAN SICE MARIMBA MALLETS

ROBERT VAN SICE Robert Van Sice is one of the most exciting marimbists on today's contemporary concert scene, as well as a sought after teacher/clinician. He has performed in 35 countries, and appeared as a soloist with ensembles such as the London Sinfonietta, the Ensemble Contrechamps, and in broadcasts for the BBC, German Radio, and Radio France. Mr. Van Sice has released three CD's on the Etcetera label and is presently under contract with Made Records in New York.

Synthetic core models have a very colorful, light, "singing" sound. Rubber core models are slightly heavier and create a more monotonal, fundamental sound. Mallet heads are secured with 20 interlocking stitches which work together to better maintain the shape and integrity of the head, while our exclusive hand-wrapping technique virtually eliminates the sound of bar contact. Handles are first quality rock maple 17" long with rounded butt ends and waxed finish for maximum playing comfort. NOTE: All Robert Van Sice marimba mallets are digitally weight-matched in sets of four, instead of pairs, to ensure an evenly balanced grouping.

TX739W   Evelyn Glennie

TX740W   Evelyn Glennie

EG1 Soft Core   (Cord Wrapped)

EG3 Medium Core (Cord Wrapped)

EG5 Hard Core   (Cord Wrapped)

Synthetic Core   (Yarn Wrapped)

Rubber Core   (Yarn Wrapped)

Robert Van Sice Marimba Mallets by Pro-Mark

Model	Sound Characteristics	Core
VSM1	Very dark (Bass marimba)	Synthetic
VSM2	Dark	Synthetic
VSM3	Medium dark-Medium bright	Synthetic
VSM4	Medium bright-Bright	Synthetic
VSM5	Medium bright-Very bright	Synthetic
VSM6	Bright-Very bright	Synthetic
VSM77	2-Tone. Dark to bright	Synthetic
VSM88	2-Tone. Dark to very bright	Synthetic
VSM12	Dark	Rubber
VSM13	Medium dark	Rubber
VSM14	Medium bright	Rubber
VSM15	Bright	Rubber
VSM16	Very bright	Rubber

Specifications are subject to change.

Creative Firm   **Talbot Design Group**
                          Westlake Village, California
Client   *Griffin Industries*

This 14" x 7" brochure is bound with a twig and elastic
band. Except for two vellum sheets, all pages are printed on
different recycled papers. Metallic ink is used on the
vellum.

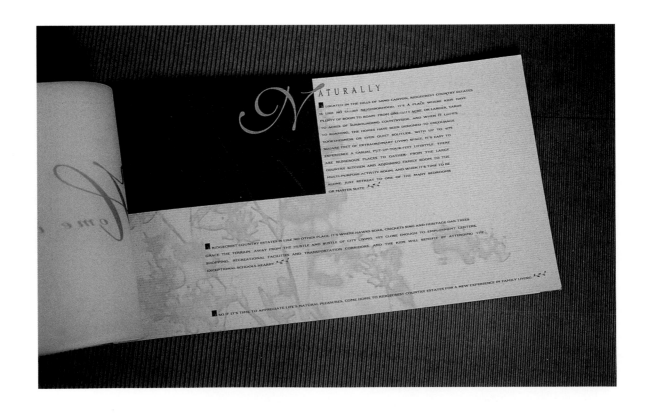

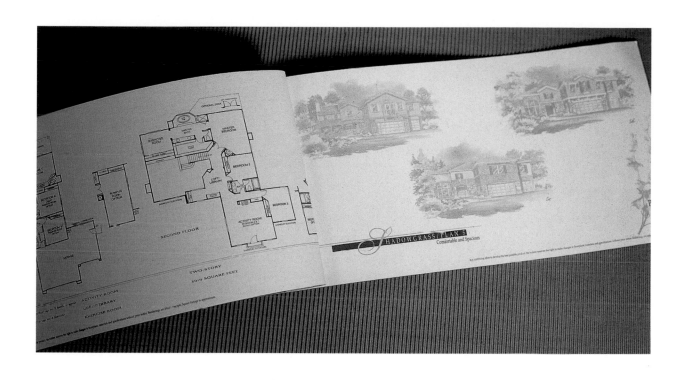

Creative Firm   **Dunn and Rice Design**
Rochester, New York
Client   *Dunn and Rice Design*

Folded brochure uses four-color process and varnish printing. Closed, it measures 8" x 14".
Completely open, it's 32" x 14".

Strategic corporate communications and results-driven product marketing are the foundations of a **successful business.** Dunn and Rice Design is a graphic design and marketing consultation firm committed to these principles. We create communications that capture the character, culture and heart of your business— great design that produces **great results** for a growing list of regional and national clients.

Great design doesn't happen on its own. Great design is aesthetics meeting purpose, strategy, and **vision.** It's accomplished by listening to who you are, what you're about and understanding what you've got to say and what you've got to sell. It's knowing what makes your audience tick and synthesizing the information into communications that demand **action.** Like a locomotive racing around a bend, it smacks your audience square between the baby blues. **It inspires. It motivates.**

Dunn and Rice Design provides **comprehensive and strategic** corporate communications including: corporate identities, annual reports, capability brochures, brand identities, packaging, environmental graphics, exhibits, displays and web-sites. We also develop strategy for merchandising including planogram development and provide marketing research and copywriting services.

Inside you'll see a small sampling of our work—just enough to whet your appetite. If you're interested in seeing more or would like to talk to us about a problem you need **solved,** pick up the phone and give us a shout. We look forward to working with you.

...caring about a brand, it touches your audience square between the baby blues. **It inspires. It motivates.**

Dunn and Rice Design provides **compre-hensive and strategic** corporate communications including corporate identities, annual reports, capability brochures, brand identities, packaging, environmental graphics, exhibits, displays and web sites. We also develop strategy for merchandising including planogram development and provide marketing research and copywriting services.

Inside, you'll find a small sampling of our work—just enough to whet your appetite. If you're interested in seeing more or would like to talk to us about a problem you need **solved**, pick up the phone and give us a shout. We look forward to working with you.

Saab 9000

A Technical Overview

1996

Find your own road.™

SAAB

Creative Firm   **RMI, Inc.**
       Emerson, New Jersey
Client   *Saab Cars USA, Inc.*

White glossy cover stock is used for text pages in this 9-1/4" x 12" spiral-bound brochure. Cover itself is very heavy white board. Die-cut inside pages offer topical tabs on outside edges.

All Weather Driving

Saab 9000

What makes the Saab 9000 an exhilarating car to drive also makes it a safe one. The way it sticks to the road. Saab cars are developed in Sweden, where the climate is cold and damp for much of the year and the roads are often treacherous with ice and snow.

Just as important as finding your own road is staying on it. The Saab 9000 Series chassis is carefully balanced between front and rear to help it hold the road. The human body is extremely sensitive to changes in the lateral forces which filter through the seat cushions. These signals warn us that we are on the verge of losing traction on sharp curves. That is why we have dimensioned our chassis so that the driver's hip is close to the car's center of gravity. This makes it easier to sense how the car is moving and speeds up the driver's reactions, which often take place by pure reflex. "Driving by the seat of one's pants" has never been truer.

Front-wheel drive and steady weight distribution combine with an aerodynamic body to ensure reliable directional stability.

Safe cars need reliable brakes. All Saab cars for many years now have featured disc brakes on all four wheels. And in front they are ventilated to prevent fading during repeated hard use - good foundation for an efficient ABS system.

A good car communicates with the driver in a variety of ways, for example, via the steering wheel, pedal and seat. Contact with the road becomes a natural extension of contact between the car and driver.

Intelligent chassis design gives Saab cars sports car roadhandling. This translates into abundant driving pleasure combined with generous safety margins in everyday driving.

The safe driving characteristics of Saab cars stem not only from front-wheel drive and optimized chassis geometry, but also from even and consistent weight distribution. With the driver aboard, roughly 60% of the weight is over the front wheels and 40% over the rear. This changes to roughly 50/50 with a fully loaded car.

60%   40%

The Anti-lock Braking System means each wheel has a sensor which registers whether the wheel is rotating or about to lock. Before it can lock, the ABS system instantly releases and reapplies brake pressure. ABS is a standard feature on all Saabs.

ABS (Anti-Lock Braking System) prevents the wheels from locking, no matter how hard you push the brake pedal. ABS allows the brakes to be applied to the very verge of locking, which means that the braking distance is reduced while still retaining steering control.

When the ABS sensors indicate that a moving wheel is about to lose its grip and begin to spin, the TCS system gently reduces power with the help of an extra throttle shutter in the engine until traction is regained. If necessary, simply disengage the system by pressing a button.

Trusting the all-weather capabilities of their fleets of Saab 9000s, both the Aspen and Vail police tear through snow storms as well as the summer heat of mountain passes.

ABS

Where Our Road Began.

Right from the start, Saab's cars have been designed and produced by people with strong personalities. Independent individuals, with the courage to question what is established, rely on their intuition and go their own way to create something beyond the conventional. It was an unconventional approach to designing an automobile, but it produced a very practical solution.

And, consequently, these are exactly the sort of people for whom we build our cars. Intelligent, questioning individuals, who do not hesitate to choose the unconventional when it is advantageous to do so.

The form-follows function approach has given our cars their characteristics since the first Saab saw the light of day.

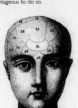

Our designers have retained the unique identity while taking functionality a step further with each model. From the aerodynamic prototype 92001 in 1946, the Saab 92 in 1949 through Saab Sonett I, II and III, Saab 95, and Saab 9000 — all milestones on the road to today's impressive model range.

Saab 9000 CS

Saab 9000 Aero

Saab 9000 CSE

Today's Saabs are designed to meet all the stringent demands placed on cars in our society. As you get to know them better, you will see that they retain their original soul and typical Saab character. The result is a line of cars with unique style and performance, designed for people who prefer striking out on a different path.

Every Saab is built to be experienced from behind the wheel, out on the road. The Saab 9000 is no exception. No matter which model you choose - CS, CSE or Aero - you'll be driving a car created from genuine insight into the interaction between car and driver.

All cars in the Saab 9000 Series are a pleasure to drive, individual in design, safe and respectful of the environment. Affordable cars offering real performance and responsibility.

Out of a spirit of innovation comes a road all your own. Because to express individuality, you don't follow others. You find your own road.

Reliability

When it comes to reliability, others have plenty to say about Saab. There's the 9000 Series awards from *Consumer Review* and *The Car Book*, which named the 9000 a "Best Bet" due to its safety, low insurance premiums and low preventive maintenance costs. Maintenance costs so low that, historically, the average cost for a Saab service visit, as reported in *Auto Week*, is among the lowest in its class.

For additional proof of Saab reliability, we point to our warranty (one that other cars with reputations for reliability, like Honda Accord Ex and Nissan Maxima SE can't match). You can enjoy peace-of-mind knowing that you're covered by one of the finest warranties in the industry. The Saab New Car Warranty includes:
◆ Bumper-to-Bumper coverage for 4 years or 50,000 miles.*
◆ Adjustments and wear item coverage for 1 full year or 16,000 miles.*
◆ Safety belt and supplemental restraint system coverage for 5 years, unlimited mileage.
◆ Perforation warranty for 6 years, unlimited mileage.

The Saab 9000 is built by individualists, for individualists. It offers the typical Saab combination of performance, safety, comfort and driving pleasure.

Saab 9000 Aero

Saab 9000 CSE

Saab 9000 CSE

Awards

Saab 9000

The many awards of the Saab 9000 prove that Saab, although one of the world's smallest car manufacturers, is among the leaders in terms of technical innovation, design, safety and environment respect.

"Lowest vehicle fatalities for any car in production" *Insurance Institute for Highway Safety, 1995*
"Best Theft Protection Prize"
(Saab 9000) NRMA, Insurance, Australia, 1995.
"Top Ten Engines of 1995"
(Saab 2.3-liter LPT) Ward's Auto World/Ward's Engine Technology & Vehicle Update Magazine, USA 1995.
"Safest car on the market 1993/94"
Folksam Insurance Company, Sweden, 1994.
"Best Performance Car of The Year"
(Saab 9000 Aero) Car News, Taiwan, 1994.
"Alternate Law Enforcement Car"
Police Magazine, USA, 1994.
"Substantially better than average" for injury losses (all 9000s) *Highway Loss Data, Data Institute (HLDI)*
"Technology Of The Year"
(Saab Trionic) Automobile Magazine, USA, 1993.
"Top Car In Its Price Class" *(Saab 9000CS) American Automobile Association, USA, 1993.*
"9000 Aero Leads EPA Large Car Fuel Economy" *Environmental Protection Agency (EPA), USA, 1993-1994.*
"Top 40 Best Car"
Consumer Review Magazine, USA, 1993.
"Best Crash Test Index"
The Car Book, USA, 1993.
"Technological Innovation Prize '93"
(Saab Trionic) Motoring Journalist's Club of Denmark, 1993.
"Best Design — Saab 9000 Aero"
Svensk Form, Sweden, 1993.
"Best Bet" *The Car Book, USA 1993,1994, & 1995.*
"Class Win, Michelin Downeast Tour"
Rally and Sports Car Club of America, USA, 1992.
"Safest Car On The Market, 1991/92"
Folksam Insurance Company, Sweden, 1992.
"Most Environmentally Friendly Car In Its Class"
German Medical Magazine "Status", Germany, 1992.
"Safest Car On The Market 1989/90"
Folksam Insurance Company, Sweden, 1990.

* Whichever comes first. See your Saab dealer for details about this limited warranty.

If you should experience car trouble, help is just a phone call away with Saab Roadside Assistance. Dial our toll-free number for emergency assistance 24 hours a day, 365 days a year, anywhere in the United States. Best of all, it's yours at no additional charge for 4 years or 50,000 miles.*

We created the Saab Dedicated Delivery System® to ensure that you and your new car get off to a fantastic start. Your car will be thoroughly cleaned, prepared and inspected. And your dealer will be happy to spend time familiarizing you with the 9000's full array of features. After 5,000 miles, your first scheduled maintenance is free.

And when you need repairs, your local authorized Saab dealer is the place to go. Only Saab service technicians receive on-going training and continuous updates on Saab service, methods, diagnostic tools and technology.

In short, you can count on Saab's commitment to superior service from the moment you step into a Saab showroom and throughout your entire ownership.

Creative Firm   **ID Incorporated**
                 Portland, Oregon
Client   *Portland Software*

White matte papers of different weights were used for this brochure's cover and interior. The cover, though included in the spiral binding, is constructed much like a box to protect its contents. Inside, tab pages are die-cut for easy info access. Printed on card stock, a metallic-looking band holds this 9-1/4" x 11" package together.

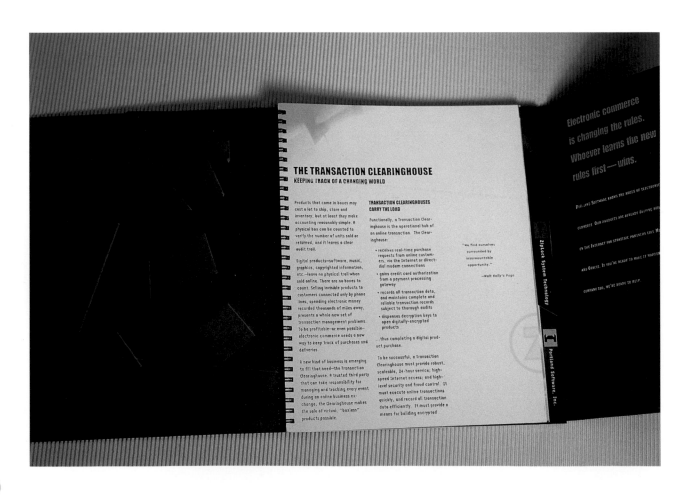

39

Seeing
clearly

THE **FOLLETT SOFTWARE COMPANY** VISION

Creative Firm   **Esdale Associates, Inc.**
               Chicago, Illinois
Client   *Follett Software Company*

Cover consists of heavy vellum, printed and die cut to show card stock underneath. Back cover is textured navy with an inside pocket. Spiral-binding lends itself to some pages being perfectly bound. Two text papers are used inside: textured, fibered tan, and matte white. Overall measurement is 9" x 11-1/2".

Insight

At Follett Software Company, we value our role in education. We work *with* you in a true partnership. We're doing business with more insight, and more understanding. Because we know that, together with educators, we can make a difference in the way people learn.

Where does our insight come from? We start with a partnership with librarians, who are at the grass roots of education and the heart of our work — because librarians are so involved with technology, transforming libraries and learning. We spend time out in the field, working with librarians where education happens. We try to keep the details and the big picture in sight at all times. We truly understand what our customers need, because we ask them. It's that simple. The involvement of librarians is key to every union, every data conversion, every on-line public access catalog, and every circulation system. So it only makes sense that our company also employs librarians, right alongside the people who develop the technology that performs in today's libraries and schools.

Follett Software Company works to advance the cause of collaboration between librarians and teachers, with networking tools that connect classrooms with libraries, and curriculum products that succeed with librarians, teachers, and students alike. The idea of connection extends to our efforts on a larger scale, as more and more school districts

and library unions choose Follett Software Company. For everyone from technology coordinators to district administrators, we create the solutions that make the most practical sense and the biggest contribution to the goals of education. And our technology is designed to work *for* students and patrons, making the process of accessing information and acquiring skills as natural and easy and enjoyable as possible. The way we see it, a productive relationship with the people we educate is the most meaningful and rewarding partnership of all.

Follett Software Company offers practical solutions. More importantly, we see the concepts that give all the solutions and technology meaning. Everything we do, from addressing issues of connectivity, Internet access, WANs, and quality data, to efforts directly related to information literacy and technology integration, is ultimately about information access and lifelong learning. The library is where information access happens and lifelong learning starts. That is what we all want to advance. Follett Software Company will help bring your library or district to the level you hope to reach. We take you where you want to be.

Chuck Follett

Work with a trusted partner as you develop a district-level technology plan that inspires confidence.

AND THEN RELAX.

Seeing The Importance Of Data

Data makes all the difference. The library user relies on quality data to help find the right material. At Follett Software Company, we keep the importance of data in mind at all times as we work to build better library automation solutions. Our software works to manage your records as intelligently and easily as possible. And the records generated by Follett Software Company meet the highest quality standard.

Follett Software Company's Data Services department handles the labor-intensive retrospective card conversion process, enabling a library's records to comply with the important MARC standard while freeing a librarian's time to dedicate to education and serving patrons. We lead the industry in producing enhanced MARC (MAchine Readable Cataloging) records for K-12 libraries. And the enhanced records we create include more access points to help patrons identify a title based on interest or reading levels, or keywords. The electronic records we convert include summary and content notes to help patrons determine which titles best suit their needs. We built our database over the course of more than 20 years, so we have a greater number of enhanced records than anyone else. While other vendors simply distribute Library of Congress records, Follett Software Company adds the data that helps patrons access information.

Authority Control Processing from Follett Software Company assists in ongoing collection management with standardized headings.

Authority records that match your headings produce See and See Also cross-references — yet another way to help patrons search with more precision and focus.

Follett Software Company is one of the field's leaders in responding to the Curriculum Enhanced MARC (CEMARC) standard. Curriculum Enhanced MARC records standardize the link between the school curriculum and the school library's collection, helping educators quickly and easily locate high-quality resources to address specific needs in the classroom.

A partnership with Follett Software Company means a greater ability to generate and manage your all-important data. Your patrons will find information more efficiently and successfully.

Follett Software Company believes in the intrinsic value of technology to help attain the goals of education. In support of that commitment, the company and its employees belong to the following worthy organizations.
ALA (American Library Association)
AASL (American Association of School Libraries)
LITA (Library and Information Technology Association)
ALCTS (Association for Library Collections and Technical Services)
OLAC Inc. (On-line Audiovisual Catalogers, Inc.)
MicroLIF Committee
Chicago Software Publishers Association
ASIS (American Society of Information Sciences)
SPIN (Chicago Software Process Improvement Network)
USMARC Advisory Group
TLA (Texas Library Association), PSLA (Pennsylvania Library Association), and many other local library groups

Technology should be user-friendly, and easy to manage at the same time.

WE'LL WORK WITH YOU
to develop the right solution.

How We View Networking

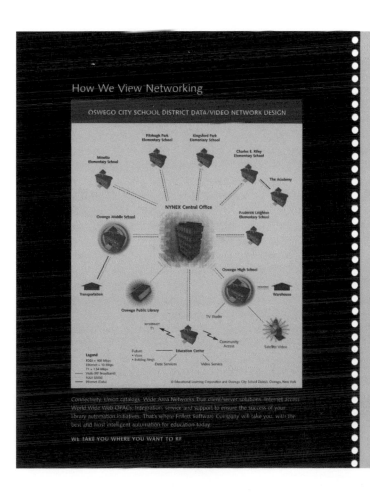

OSWEGO CITY SCHOOL DISTRICT DATA/VIDEO NETWORK DESIGN

Fitzhugh Park Elementary School
Kingsford Park Elementary School
Charles E. Riley Elementary School
Minetto Elementary School
The Academy
Frederick Leighton Elementary School
NYNEX Central Office
Oswego Middle School
Transportation
Oswego High School
Warehouse
Oswego Public Library
TV Studio
Community Access
Satellite Video
Future Education Center
Data Services
Video Service

Legend
FDDI = 100 Mbps
Ethernet = 10 Mbps
T1 = 1.54 Mbps

© Educational Learning Corporation and Oswego City School District, Oswego, New York

Connectivity. Union catalogs. Wide Area Networks. True client/server solutions. Internet access. World Wide Web OPACs. Integration, service and support to ensure the success of your library automation initiatives. That's where Follett Software Company will take you. With the best and most intelligent automation for education today.

WE TAKE YOU WHERE YOU WANT TO BE

Automation: A Checklist

From helpful guidance at the conceptual stages of your automation process, through training and data conversion, along with software, hardware, integration and installation, Follett Software Company can be your partner. We'll work at your side through every step of the process.

- Create a vision of what you want your system to achieve.
- Learn everything you can about automation, through reading, conferences, workshops, even field trips.
- Get input from your colleagues, with a worksheet assessing needs.
- Define your connectivity goals and how they'll affect infrastructure.
- Develop a statement describing the system you're planning and your expectations.
- Prepare your plan, with a timeline and funding proposal.
- Present your proposal to administrators, staff, and potential funding sources.
- Win approval and proceed!
- Purchase your software.
- Purchase your hardware and peripheral equipment.
- Arrange for integration and installation.
- Order supplies, such as patron cards and barcode labels.
- Choose your approach for converting your card catalog to MARC records.
- Prepare to convert your data; conduct an inventory and review shelflist cards for missing information.
- Assemble a team to barcode your collection.
- Oversee installation.
- Review the system before you enter data.
- Arrange training for yourself and your staff.
- Plan the introduction of the system to students and patrons.
- Schedule a faculty in-service day on information technology and the curriculum.
- Follow up after a few months and evaluate the implementation of your technology plan.

Follett Software Company Solutions

A relationship of understanding and trust. An awareness of the importance of information skills and high-quality data. A shared goal of improving education by all the means available in a time of technological change. This way of working with educators, and this view of our place in the world of education, shows in every product and each service offered by today's Follett Software Company.

intelligent
a u t o m a t i o n

Creative Firm **Mires Design**
San Diego, California
Client *Food Group*

White glossy cover stock is used for this folded 8" x 10-3/4" brochure.

42

Creative Firm   **Eric Chan Design Co. Ltd.**
Hong Kong, China
Client   *Italian Trade Commission*

Leather-grained card stock makes the cover for this 5-3/4" x 8-1/4" brochure all tied
together with a shoe lace.

Creative Firm   **HEBE. Werbung & Design**
                Leonberg, Germany
Client   *Regent*

Both cover and text pages are printed on
white matte stock. Cover includes gold foil
stamping and pinked inside flaps. Silver and
gold metallic inks are used intermittently
inside.

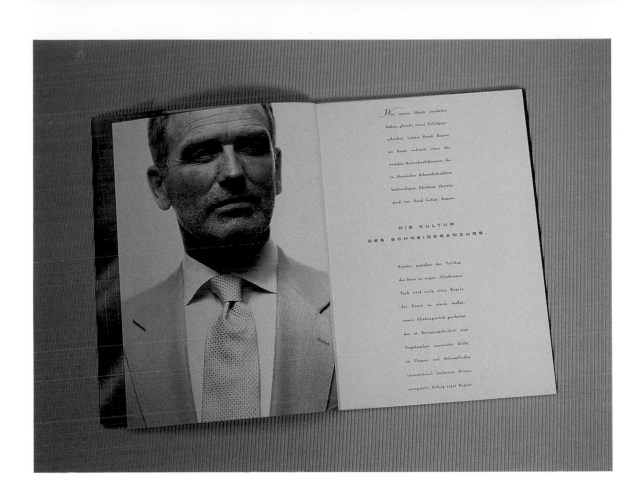

45

snap·shot (snap′shot′), *n.*, *v.*,
1. an informal photograph.
2. *Informal.* a brief appraisal,
summary or profile.

Creative Firm   **Gerstman+Meyers**
                 New York, New York
Client   *Gerstman+Meyers*

Wide brochure, 9-1/4" x 4", is spiral-bound. All pages are printed on one side only. Stock is white glossy with a heavier weight used for the cover.

46

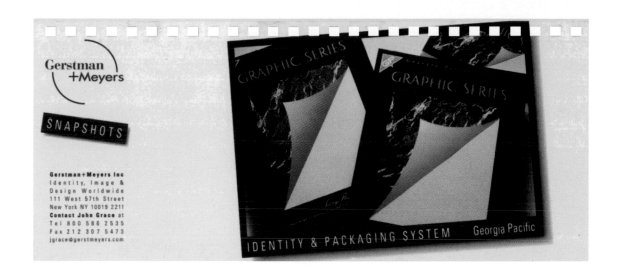

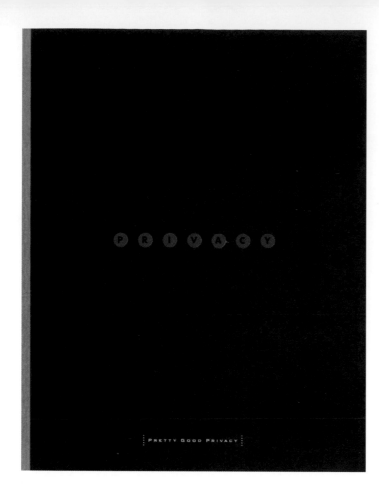

PRIVACY

PRETTY GOOD PRIVACY

Creative Firm   **Hornall Anderson Design Works, Inc.**
                 Seattle, Washington
Client   *PGP*
                 (Pretty Good Privacy)

Inside white matte sheets are heavier stock than the cover. Cover uses round die cuts for a see-through effect. Back inside cover offers a curved-edge pocket with cuts that will hold a business card. Overall size is 9" x 11-1/2".

Restoring privacy in the information age

Pretty Good Privacy, Inc.™ provides a broad range of privacy solutions that prevent the risk of unauthorized access to digital property.

Secure your digital property with privacy solutions from Pretty Good Privacy, Inc.

PRETTY GOOD PRIVACY, INC. PROVIDES a broad range of privacy solutions that prevent the risk of unauthorized access to digital property. The company's software products ensure privacy for both companies and individuals.

PRETTY GOOD HISTORY

The original Pretty Good Privacy product, PGP, made its debut as freeware in 1991. Privacy rights activist Philip Zimmermann introduced the product to protest an impending government mandate that would have forced manufacturers of encryption software to design special "back doors" that would enable the government to read encrypted messages.

PGP gathered grass-roots support as software engineers volunteered their assistance in enhancing the software. The company incorporated as Pretty Good Privacy, Inc. in March, 1996 to market commercial versions of what has become the most popular e-mail encryption software available.

ENCRYPTION FOR EVERYONE—NOT JUST EXPERTS

Traditionally, powerful encryption technology has been limited to military and technical users because the cryptographic algorithms were restricted and the user interfaces arcane. Pretty Good Privacy designs its products to be accessible by all computer users. The technology is strong enough for the most rigorous security requirements; the interface simple enough for casual users.

A key differentiator for Pretty Good Privacy is that its products and services are not bound to a particular platform, operating system, application, or algorithm. The company delivers independent privacy solutions suited for heterogeneous networks. All products are designed to work smoothly with related Internet applications, such as e-mail and browsers.

THE THREE FACETS OF PRIVACY

Privacy has three facets: encryption, authentication, and anonymity. Pretty Good Privacy offers products and services that satisfy each.

Encryption: Clothing naked data

"They undercut every aspect of our proposal. How could they have known?"

Secure communications relies on encryption, which prevents anyone from reading files intercepted in transit or stored locally. There are two popular encryption methods. In the secret key method, both parties use the same key, an impractical alternative for business people, who would need to manage a separate secret key for each of their correspondents. In the public key method, each user has a public key, which can be distributed widely, without risk, as well as a private key, which is never shared. Both are required to decrypt messages. The result: Only the person who maintains the private key can read messages intended for that person.

PGPmail, the flagship product of Pretty Good Privacy, is based on public key cryptography and has become the *de facto* standard for secure communications. Millions use the product, including more than 30% of Fortune 100 companies. The company estimates that 95% of encrypted Internet traffic is encrypted with PGP.

> **"Privacy worries vary from the collection and distribution of personal information on the World Wide Web to employers snooping on workers."**
> *Stephen Wildstrom, Business Week, 11/1/96*

Pretty Good Privacy will also provide encryption solutions for other forms of communication, such as voice, fax and video. Data is encrypted at the sender's end and decrypted at the recipient's; the transmission is meaningless if intercepted in transit.

Authentication: Introducing accountability to faceless communications

"What do you mean this e-mail order isn't from somebody in your company? We've already begun manufacturing."

In the faceless world of electronic communications, how do you know the people you are corresponding with are who they say they are, or that the person who places the order is authorized to make that decision?

Authentication means ensuring the message was originated by the person who it appears to be from, and that the message has not been electronically altered after being sent. PGPmail lets senders include a unique digital signature with their transmissions, proving they originated the transmission and it was not altered in transit.

Anonymity: Giving you freedom to explore unnoticed

"Our company appears in a list of organizations supporting Proposition A. That's against our policy."

Companies increasingly take advantage of the Web to research competitors or potential partners, download software, and order supplies. Web site operators can find out information about their visitors by reading their access logs, which contain the IP address, last site visited, and other information. With "cookie" technology, they can find out even more. The threat to privacy is far-reaching. Part of an enterprise-wide privacy plan is to ensure that company employees can take advantage of the Web for business but not give out valuable information in the process.

As one step toward anonymity, Pretty Good Privacy provides a plug-in for browser software that allows users to choose which cookies—written to their hard disks by various Web servers—to retain or discard.

Through the use of public key cryptography, PGPmail™ ensures that individuals never need to share their private key. Only the intended recipient can read a private message.

PUBLIC KEY CRYPTOGRAPHY

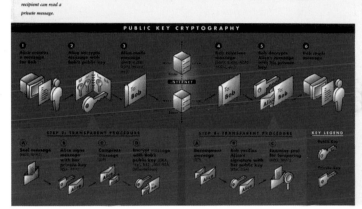

Base your privacy strategy on our strong foundation

PRETTY GOOD PRIVACY IS COMMITTED to delivering privacy solutions that are trusted and easy to use, to meet the needs of companies and individuals alike.

UNCOMPROMISED ENCRYPTION

Products from Pretty Good Privacy contain no hidden "back doors" that someone else could use to read encrypted messages. To that end, PGP publishes its source code for public review.

INTEGRATION OF MULTIPLE, LEADING TECHNOLOGIES

Pretty Good Privacy does not rely on a single algorithm. Instead, the company draws on the best cryptography available, selecting the combination of technologies best suited to a particular application.

COMMITMENT TO OPEN STANDARDS

Products from Pretty Good Privacy are written to conform to emerging industry standards and application program interfaces (APIs). The company participates in major standards-setting committees, including the Internet Engineering Task Force (IETF) and World Wide Web Consortium (W3C). Pretty Good Privacy supports the development of standards for e-mail, electronic commerce, network level encryption, and development environments.

PARTNERSHIP WITH THE BEST IN MANY INDUSTRIES

To deliver privacy throughout the enterprise, Pretty Good Privacy establishes partnerships with vendors of products used throughout the Internet, including operating systems, browsers, development environments, messaging and groupware, and telephony equipment.

CONVENIENT SERVICE AND SUPPORT

All products from Pretty Good Privacy come with technical support and documentation. Resources for marketing, sales and distribution, are available on the Web.

> **"Thanks to the Internet, personal privacy is quickly becoming a thing of the past."**
> *Margie Semilof, Communications Week, 10/28/96*

> **"Once you put a lot of information about yourself—name, address, income, hobbies and interests—on the Web, the potential exists for a massive invasion of your privacy."**
> *Walter Mossberg, Wall Street Journal, 10/24/96*

Creative Firm   **Emery Vincent Design**
                 Southbank, Canada
Client   *Emery Vincent Design*

White matte cover, 6-1/4" x 9-1/4", is printed front and back, full bleed, and offers inside flaps. Inside printing on text-weight matte white includes selectively used varnishes.

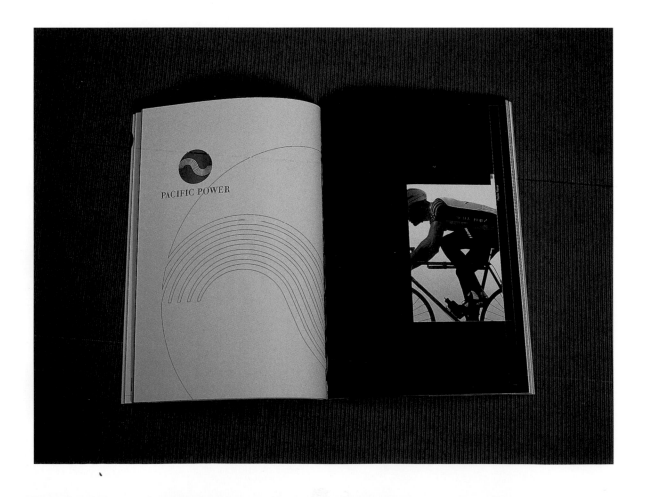

What's New?

Creative Firm **Herman Miller Communications Development**
Zeeland, Michigan

Client *Herman Miller Inc.*

Sized to hold in your hand, 4" x 8" brochure is spiral-bound. Cover and text pages use the same weight, white matte paper. Cover is printed in multiple colors, while each inside page is printed in one or two colors.

The Ambi™ chair

Building on a new understanding of customer requirements and decades of seating engineering experience, the Ambi chair offers Herman Miller-class ergonomic support and design sophistication at a very affordable price.

Based on the premise that everyone who works in the office today needs a comfortable and supportive work chair, the Ambi work chair comes standard with essential adjustments and a sophisticated CoActive™ tilt. For people who require a more personalized fit, optional adjustments like seat depth, armrest height, seat angle, tilt lock, and a lower seat-height range can be added in any combination.

With the Ambi line, there's a good fit for every body and a good chair for every budget.

The Aeron™ chair

The Aeron chair charts new territory in seating design, combining advanced materials, kinematic engineering, and sizing concepts to provide unprecedented levels of comfort and performance for the widest user population.

The chair's unique Pellicle™ suspension creates an elastic, permeable seat and backrest. Perfectly tensioned on contoured frames, the Pellicle material has a neutral effect on pressure distribution and skin surface temperatures, enhancing comfort over upholstered foam seating. Mimicking the body's natural movements, the Kinemat™ tilt maintains optimal lower back support through an unprecedented range of motion—from forward sitting to deeply reclined postures.

Proportioned in three sizes to fit physical statures from the 1st-percentile female through the 99th-percentile male, the Aeron chair also has adjustable lumbar support and pivoting, height-adjustable arms.

The Equa 2 chair with
Newhouse Group® furniture,
a Liaison® cabinet,
and the Ethospace system

To provide the same fit for varieties of work styles that our work chairs offer for varieties of body shapes and sizes, Herman Miller makes several lines of versatile freestanding furniture that can be used alone or combined with systems products to support different types of organizations and different patterns of work. Here, Newhouse Group furniture is paired with a Liaison cabinet and Ethospace components to provide adjustable computer support, customized storage, and some visual privacy in an open, team environment.

The light scale and advanced ergonomics of the Equa 2 chair make it a natural choice for this type of dynamic, multifunctional work space.

Creative Firm   **Smiley/Hanchulak, Inc.**
                 Akron, Ohio
Client   *Parker Hannifin Corporation*

Staple-bound, this 8-1/2" x 11" brochure uses the same weight, smooth, white glossy stock for cover and text pages. Varnish is used in accordance with four-color printing.

Since the 1950s, Parker has been recognized as a pioneer in aluminum impact technology. Over the last two decades, we've expanded our expertise to include the manufacturing of aluminum alloy compressed gas cylinders – known for superior features of quality and convenience.

When compared to traditional cylinders made of steel, Parker one-piece aluminum cylinders offer many advantages:

Lightweight and portable

Parker cylinders are easier to handle and up to 50 percent lighter than most steel cylinders.

Corrosion resistant

Due to their rust and corrosion resistance, our cylinders are preferred for maintaining accurate purity levels and close tolerance calibrations of gases.

Damage resistant

For maximum durability in rough applications, Parker cylinders provide a greater wall thickness than most steel cylinders.

Smooth interior

Parker's monobloc cylinder design maintains gas purity with an interior surface free of welds, seams or folds that can trap previous gases and cleaning agents.

Economical

Because of their lighter weight, our cylinders are more cost-effective and reduce shipping expenses.

Adaptable to low temperatures

Parker's aluminum alloy material withstands colder temperatures and is recommended for cryogenic service.

Flat bottom

Designed with a flat base, our cylinders are made for stable, free-standing use and more convenient storage.

Parker has the perfect fit for your application.

Our aluminum compressed gas cylinders come in a broad range of standard stock sizes – from two to 10 inches in outside diameter and up to 50 inches in length.

Made with straight threads, Parker cylinders are designed to be sealed with O-rings. Exteriors are available in brushed aluminum, or choose from our wide selection of durable, epoxy-painted finishes.

To meet your more specific needs, Parker will manufacture custom sizes to match your requirements for length, capacity, pressure rating and threads. Our representatives will work closely with you in determining how a specially designed cylinder can succeed in your application.

Superior quality control. One feature we won't alter.

Strict quality assurance is an important part of the Parker philosophy.

From the instant raw material is received, inspection documentation begins and continues throughout each step of the production process. All cylinders undergo stringent independent testing for compliance, including 100 percent

volumetric/expansion testing–executed with the most advanced equipment available today.

When it comes to cylinder integrity, Parker aluminum compressed gas cylinders are manufactured to meet or exceed the specifications of the U.S. Department of Transportation (DOT) and Transport Canada.

We offer competitive pricing, expedient service and readily available stock for immediate shipping from our high-volume production plants in Cleveland, Ohio, and Trumann, Arkansas.

Use Parker cylinders with the following gases:

Common names in parentheses

Air, compressed
Ammonia, anhydrous
Argon
Arsine
Bromochlorodifluoromethane
Bromotrifluoromethane
Carbon Dioxide, liquefied
Carbon Dioxide and Nitrous Oxide mixtures
Carbon Monoxide
Carbonyl Sulfide
Carbonyl Sulfide (Disulfide)
Chlorodifluoroethane
Chlorodifluoromethane
Chloropentafluoroethane
Chlorotrifluoromethane
Cyclopropane
Cyclobutane
Dichlorodifluoromethane
Difluoroethane
Dimethyl Ether
Diborane
Ethane
Ethylene
Freon (refrigerant gas)
Helium
Hydrogen, mercury free
Hydrogen Sulfide
Hydrocyanic Acid
Hydrogen Selinide
Krypton
Methane
Methylacetylene – Propadiene
Methyl Parathion
Neon
Nitrogen
Nitrogen Dioxide, liquid
Nitrogen Peroxide, liquid
Nitrogen Tetroxide, liquid
Nitric Oxide
Nitrous Oxide*
Oxygen*
Parathion
Phosphine
Propylene
Silane
Sulphur Dioxide
Sulphur Hexafluoride
Vinyl Chloride
Vinyl Fluoride, inhibited
Vinyl Bromide
Xenon

*Most require special cleaning in accordance with 49 CFR 173.302(a)(5)(i).

See DOT specifications for cleaning, cylinder pressure, percent of fill, valving, special shipping and all other special provisions.

The above list is generally approved for aluminum compressed gas cylinders. For specific regulations, refer to 3AL specification cylinders as listed in 49 CFR Part 173.

For end users, as well as all channels of distribution, Parker cylinders are outfitted with the features needed to facilitate a variety of applications.

Additionally, we develop market-specific programs that help make your processes more efficient and convenient. At Parker, our goal is to work with you in designing systems that bring your application to its maximum potential.

Beverage

In the beverage industry, we've introduced the first color-coded Lexan® handles with comfortable finger grips, making transportation and ownership identification much easier.

Another advantage for the beverage market is the Parker Dating System, an easy-identification labeling program for cylinders due for hydrotesting and inspection. This complete system features color-coded labels that boldly call out the year and month of the next required inspection, helping users maintain compliance with government regulations.

Industrial

At Parker, we manufacture our cylinders with thick and durable walls to withstand the rough demands of industrial environments. Designed with a flat base, they also provide stability during stationary use.

Fire

The lightweight feature of Parker cylinders is required for efficient response in fire emergencies. Available in a wide range of sizes, Parker CO₂ cylinders can be either wall- or floor-mounted for easy accessibility.

Scuba

In sport and commercial diving, Parker's aluminum material prevents interior rust and scale, keeping air clean and odor-free and paths for breathing clear. Our cylinders are manufactured to meet or exceed all aquatic safety standards and are available in many bright, gloss-painted finishes.

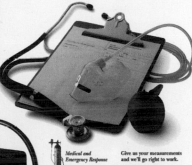

Specialty Gases and Applications

Our ever-changing technological world has created the need for highly pure specialty gases. For these specialized markets, Parker cylinders assure the greatest gas purity with a smooth, corrosion-resistant interior free of rust, scale and hidden contaminants.

Medical and Emergency Response

Because of their corrosion resistance, Parker cylinders are frequently used in the medical and emergency response environments, where purity of oxygen is vital for resuscitation, life support and respiratory therapy. Made of lightweight aluminum, Parker cylinders also provide the portability needed by ambulatory patients and emergency teams during critical situations of life and death.

Give us your measurements and we'll go right to work.

Whatever market you're in, Parker is ready to fit your needs with a standard size or custom design. Just call us with your questions and specific ordering information–800-882-2588.

We'll find you're best suited for the job.

Lexan is a registered trademark of General Electric Company.

Creative Firm   **SHR Perceptual Management**
                Scottsdale, Arizona
Client   *Innovative Thinking Conference*

Square 8-3/4" brochure is printed full-bleed black on
white matte cover stock. Inside paper is text-weight matte
cream. The first and last pages of brochure are on a card
stock to remain sturdy during "interactiveness". The front
features a fold out, while the back is a tear-off registration
form.

Creative Firm   **Nolin Larosée Design Communications inc.**
Montreal, Canada
Client   *Bauer Inc.*

Bound with extending staples so brochure can be placed in a notebook, it's sized at 7-7/8" x 10-5/8". Cover and text papers are both white matte. Inside, the viewer finds two fold-out pages.

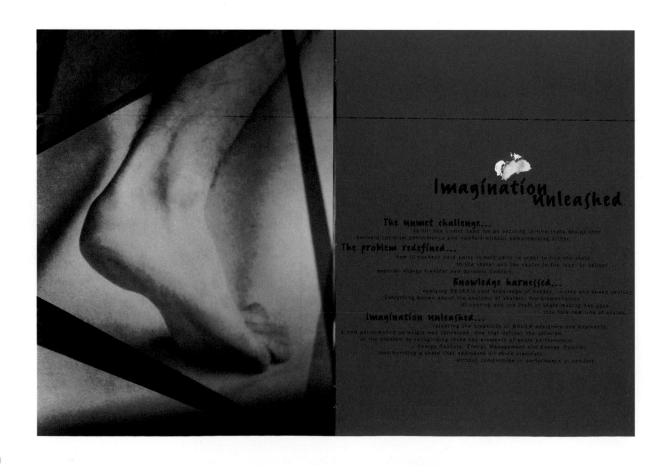

STEP — Severance Trust Executive Program — is an innovative concept in employee welfare benefits that provides severance benefits on a pre-funded, tax deductible basis. The Trust's funding utilizes life insurance contracts, thereby providing the athelete the additional benefit of life insurance.

STEP can help protect the financial security of the professional athlete while also providing powerful benefits to the sports organization.

How does a STEP program work?

The key to a STEP plan is its simplicity and its win-win structure. Here's how it works:

With the help of a benefit specialist, the program is established by the organization, which decides who to include and selects the benefit level for each participant. The organization joins the STEP Trust, makes tax deductible contributions and authorizes the Plan trustee to apply for cash value life insurance on participants. Benefits are based on contributions which can range from 2% to 10% of each participant's annual salary. (Contributions can be increased to 20% recognizing past service.)

Under the Trust agreement, the cash value can be used to pay severance benefits. The employee receives the death benefit in excess of the cash value as life insurance coverage.

When are benefits payable?

Benefits can be payable in response to a number of triggering events.

These may include:

- Death
- Disability
- Dismissal as determined by the Plan
- Dissolution or bankruptcy of the organization

Note that benefits are not payable if the athlete voluntarily quits or retires.

How does STEP benefit the athlete?

- A severance benefit can be as large as 200% of final year's compensation.

- As soon as the Plan is established, the participant is eligible for benefits upon a qualifying severance.

- Benefits are pre-funded.

- Benefits are protected from the claims of creditors, of both the athlete and the organization, until they are received.

- The lifestyle of family members can be protected through life insurance benefits payable to beneficiaries if the participant dies. Proceeds are received income tax-free. If you leave the organization, these life insurance benefits may be portable.

- Taxes are deferred on all organization contributions into the plan and investment growth until the time benefits are payable. The participant pays taxes on the term insurance costs only.

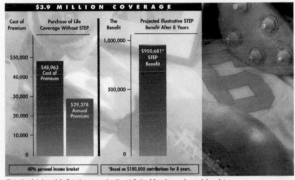

$3.9 MILLION COVERAGE

Cost of Premium	Purchase of Life Coverage Without STEP	The Benefit	Projected Illustrative STEP Benefit After 8 Years
$50,000	$48,963 Cost of Premium	1,000,000	$950,681* STEP Benefit
40,000			
30,000	$29,378 Annual Premium	500,000	
20,000			
10,000			
0		0	

| 40% personal income bracket | *Based on $100,000 contributions for 8 years. |

This is a hypothetical example for illustrative purposes only and is not indicative of the performance of any particular product.

The Professionals behind STEP

Plan Sponsor: STEP, Inc.

STEP is an important breakthrough in executive benefits; specific parameters of the Internal Revenue Code (Section 419A) may allow employers' contributions to be fully tax deductible. STEP has obtained favorable Tax and Actuarial Opinions by leading advisors in their fields.

Plan Trustee: Mellon Private Asset Management
(A service mark of Mellon Bank Corporation)

Mellon Private Asset Management provides investment management and trust services to financially successful individuals and families. Mellon ranks among the largest private asset managers in the nation with more than 125 years of experience in managing investments. Under the services of Mellon Private Asset Management, clients receive highly customized investment management and trust services designed to help them meet their individual objectives.

Legal and Tax Opinion: Jeffrey D. Mamorsky

Author of Employee Benefits Law: ERISA and Beyond (Law Journal Seminars — Press) and editor of the Employee Benefits Handbook and the Journal of Compensation and Benefits (Warren, Gorham and Lamont). Jeffrey is a partner in the international law firm of Curtis, Mallet-Prevost, Colt & Mosle in New York City. He holds a B.A. and LL.M in Taxation from New York University and a J.D. from New York Law School. On numerous occasions Mr. Mamorsky's work in the employee benefits area has been cited as an authority by the U.S. Supreme Court and other Federal and State courts.

Mr. Mamorsky authored the opinion (among other issues) that STEP's plan design allows for the deductibility of employer contributions in pre-funding for employee benefits available through STEP.

Actuarial Opinion: Ira Cohen

Ira Cohen is a former Director in the Technical and Actuarial Division of the IRS. While at the IRS, Mr. Cohen participated in the design and implementation of major tax legislation such as ERISA, TEFRA and REA. He has provided tax opinions on a wide variety of subjects, which have generated tax planning and employee benefit planning opportunities for all types of employers.

Mr. Cohen authored the favorable funding opinion that STEP's plan design does not experience rate individual employers.

Plan Independent Fiduciary: Jules Pagano

Jules Pagano is former chairman of the New York State Unemployment Commission (1981-1987), former Chairman of the Unemployment Insurance Appeals Board of the State of New York, former Chief Administrative Law Judge, and past President of the National Appellate Boards.

Mr. Pagano is STEP's Independent Fiduciary for the purpose of determining eligibility for benefits.

Is a STEP plan right for you?

STEP puts the athlete and the organization on a winning team because it is pre-funded, deductible, deferred, selective, and secured. Is STEP right for you? Only you can decide.

For more information, contact a New York Life representative at 1-800-471-3417.

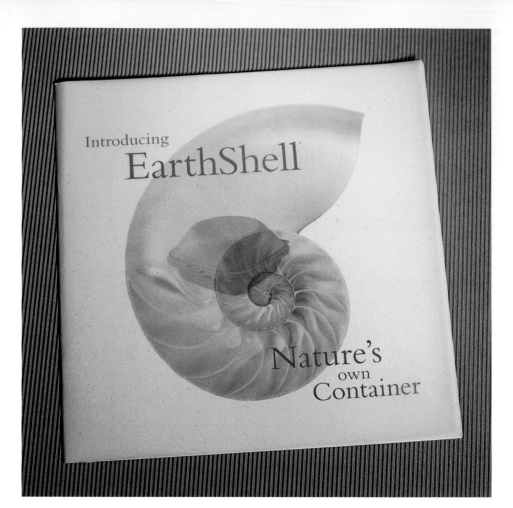

Creative Firm   **Hornall Anderson Design Works, Inc.**
Seattle, Washington
Client   *EarthShell Container Corporation*

Two-part, 11-1/4" square cover consists of printed vellum over white matte card stock. Inside is white matte text weight. Binding is stapled.

The ingredients in EarthShell are common and abundant. They're easy and inexpensive to procure. That's good news, given the world's increasing demand for take-out food (and the packaging that accompanies it).

Conserving

Every year, thousands of trees and millions of barrels of oil are used to make products we simply throw away. Can you imagine, when you order something "to go," how much else goes with it?

This, then, is the alternative EarthShell offers. If only 15% of the disposable food containers used each year in the U.S. were made of EarthShell® material rather than paper, about 100,000 trees and enough energy to power 5,000 cars annually would be saved.

Given that our need for disposable packaging will never (it seems) cut it nice to deliver a product that will in the presence of moisture last as the EarthShell® sandwich container is biodegradable in your back yard.

biodegradable

It can be composted in a back yard compost pile, and used as a soil conditioner to nourish gardens and fields. EarthShell is also compostable in commercial composting plants, which at present are very limited in number, but growing year by year.

Though modern landfills are designed to prevent biodegradation, University of Arizona research shows EarthShell® sandwich packaging will compact easily to occupy a volume similar to paper and polystyrene products.

MONEY THAT WORKS

CAPTURING THE
ENTREPRENEURIAL SPIRIT

Creative Firm   **David Slavin Design**
Los Angeles, California
Client   *Commercial Finance Association*

White glossy stocks are used in this brochure that measures
8-1/2" x 11". Back inside cover has a diagonal-edged pocket to
house extra information, and cuts to hold a business card.

ABOUT THE
COMMERCIAL FINANCE ASSOCIATION

Founded in 1944, CFA is a trade association with members
throughout the U.S., Canada and around the world. Members
include the asset-based lending arms of domestic and foreign
commercial banks, small and large independent finance companies, floor
plan financing organizations, factoring organizations and financing
subsidiaries of major industrial corporations.

CFA members play a vital part in financing the economy and are
dedicated to the growth and well-being of their clients. They provide their
clients with cash by lending on fixed assets, accounts receivable and
inventory, and engage in factoring, purchase order financing, real estate
financing and leasing.

Expert in all facets of collateralized lending, CFA member
organizations – large and small alike – possess the experience and
know-how to structure the proper financing program for their borrowers.

Backing up the practical hands-on applications of the members is the
Commercial Finance Association itself. The Association conducts ongoing
educational programs, publishes the only magazine devoted exclusively
to asset-based lending and provides updates and analyses of legal and
judicial developments that affect the lending and business communities.

GROWTH MONEY

Businesses need money to grow. A business cannot survive just
because it has a better product, an exclusive market or the best
method of distribution. The catalyst required for progress is money.

Business owners and managers must be knowledgeable about financing,
what it can do, why one form may be better than another. It can be used when:

▷ Operating cash is tied up in receivables
▷ The best trade terms for supplies create cash flow shortages
▷ Inventory levels are high because of client demands
▷ Sales growth is straining resources
▷ Seasonality peaks cause problems
▷ No fixed assets are available for collateral
▷ Trade discounts and special pricing terms cannot be obtained
▷ Letters of credit are required to supply or buy overseas
▷ Debtor-in-possession financing is required

CFA members often advance funds when traditional sources are not
available. They are familiar with various types of businesses and are
responsive to client needs.

2

3

LOAN SIZE

CFA members fund businesses with annual sales from $250,000 to more than $1 billion. Credit depends on the type of business and the content and quality of the collateral. Frequently, the credit granted is more than the net worth of the business.

The increased cash availability provided by asset-based lenders often makes the difference between profitable growth and failure for the undercapitalized business.

The phrases "too small," "too new," and "not enough net worth," do not deter an asset-based funding source.

Over the years, the list of companies that have used, and are using, asset-based financing reads like a "Who's Who" of the business world. The flexibility and availability provided by asset-based financing have enabled countless companies to grow and take advantage of market opportunities.

COST

The cost of asset-based loans is influenced by the credit risk and collateral associated with the transaction. When evaluating an asset-based loan, borrowers should assess the cost of financing in the context of the benefits to be received. Compared with other financing alternatives, asset-based lending is very cost effective and efficient.

Asset-based lenders frequently look beyond financial statements to determine how much money they are prepared to advance at and after closing. Therefore, borrowers can take advantage of profit opportunities in the market by being able to plan ahead based on their cash availability.

Asset-based lenders are proactive rather than reactive and can often restructure debt during tough times to help avoid costly and disruptive refinancing.

Over the long haul, the benefits will tend to offset the premiums associated with borrowing from the asset-based financial services industry.

TYPES OF
ASSET-BASED FINANCING

Secured lending:
The lender provides funds secured by the assets of the borrower. The collateral can include: accounts receivable, inventory, machinery, real estate, patents, trademarks or other assets where value can be determined.

The secured lender may establish a revolving loan where the borrower provides a pool of collateral that the lender translates into operating cash or working capital. The borrower uses the financing to buy more materials, expand marketing, improve productivity or other improvements and sells the resultant product. The sales create receivables that are pledged for cash advances and the payments received on the invoices pay down the loan. These increases and reductions in the loan balance are cyclical, hence the revolving nature of the loan.

Some receivables have less collateral value; for example: progress billing, past due receivables, and receivables subject to "set-off". Raw materials and finished goods are normally acceptable collateral, but work-in-progress generally is not. Equipment and real estate may also be used as a source of financing.

Non-recourse factoring:
The financing institution buys the receivable and assumes the risk of customer credit. The factor guarantees against credit loss, unlike a secured lending facility. The factor will also check credit, undertake collection and manage bookkeeping functions.

TYPES OF
ASSET-BASED FINANCING (continued)

Full-recourse factoring:
The financing institution accepts assignment of the receivable but does not assume the credit risk. The client retains responsibility for managing the receivable portfolio. Generally, the lender will finance invoices up to ninety days from delivery of goods or services, then charge them back to the client.

Discount factoring:
The factor purchases the receivables at a discount to compensate for paying prior to the due date.

Maturity factoring:
The factor purchases the receivables, assumes the credit risk and advances cash to the client as the invoices mature.

Non-notification factoring:
Account debtors are not notified of the sale of the receivables and the invoices are either paid to a lock-box or to the shipper. This is similar to a receivable loan.

Notification factoring:
Account debtors are notified of the purchase of the receivables and are directed to make payments to the factor.

Spot factoring:
A "one-shot" transaction, generally out of the normal course of business.

Creative Firm   **Laurie Kelliher**
   New York, New York
Client   *Nick International*

Very sturdy 5-3/4" x 11-1/2" brochure uses a typical white cover stock for text pages. Cover is printed on white board. Some inside pages have foldouts.

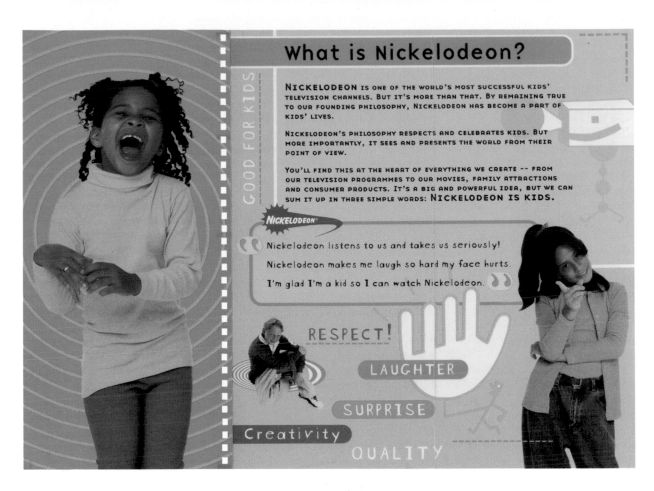

What is Nickelodeon?

NICKELODEON IS ONE OF THE WORLD'S MOST SUCCESSFUL KIDS' TELEVISION CHANNELS. BUT IT'S MORE THAN THAT. BY REMAINING TRUE TO OUR FOUNDING PHILOSOPHY, NICKELODEON HAS BECOME A PART OF KIDS' LIVES.

NICKELODEON'S PHILOSOPHY RESPECTS AND CELEBRATES KIDS. BUT MORE IMPORTANTLY, IT SEES AND PRESENTS THE WORLD FROM THEIR POINT OF VIEW.

YOU'LL FIND THIS AT THE HEART OF EVERYTHING WE CREATE -- FROM OUR TELEVISION PROGRAMMES TO OUR MOVIES, FAMILY ATTRACTIONS AND CONSUMER PRODUCTS. IT'S A BIG AND POWERFUL IDEA, BUT WE CAN SUM IT UP IN THREE SIMPLE WORDS: NICKELODEON IS KIDS.

NICKELODEON

"Nickelodeon listens to us and takes us seriously!

Nickelodeon makes me laugh so hard my face hurts.

I'm glad I'm a kid so I can watch Nickelodeon."

RESPECT!

LAUGHTER

SURPRISE

Creativity

QUALITY

NICKELODEON IS WORLDWIDE.

NICKELODEON IS GROWING.

NICKELODEON IS KIDS.

THE TRUE ESSENCE OF NICKELODEON CAN'T BE CAPTURED IN A BROCHURE OR A SALES TAPE. TO FIND IT, LOOK INSTEAD TO THE FACES OF KIDS WATCHING OUR AWARD-WINNING PROGRAMMES LIKE RUGRATS OR GLOBAL GUTS OR CLARISSA.

THEY AREN'T JUST ENTERTAINED. THEY'RE INVOLVED. NICKELODEON HAS THE POWER TO CONNECT KIDS -- WITH PROGRAMMES, WITH OTHER KIDS, AND WITH THEIR WORLD.

NICKELODEON IS THE KID EXPERT. AND IN THE LOCAL LANGUAGES OF MORE THAN 70 COUNTRIES--NICKELODEON IS KIDS.

NICKELODEON

73

Creative Firm   **Emerson, Wajdowicz
Studios**
New York, New York

Client   *Island Paper Mills,*
division of *E.B. Eddy
Forest Products Ltd.*

Printed on Bravo white gloss in 80 lb.
and 100 lb. text and cover weights,
this brochure measures 10-1/2" x
14". Back cover includes fold-out
flap with rectangular die cut.

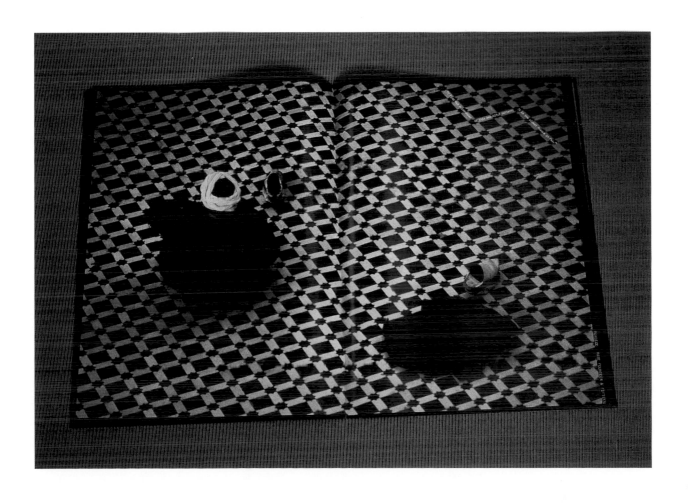

Creative Firm   **Sive/Young & Rubicam**
                        Cincinnati, Ohio
Client   *Murray Bikes*

Narrow brochure measures 4" x 9-1/4".
Cover is printed on a fibered, off-white
stock. Back inside cover has full-size,
fold-out flap. Text pages are smooth
white paper. Brochure is spiral-bound.

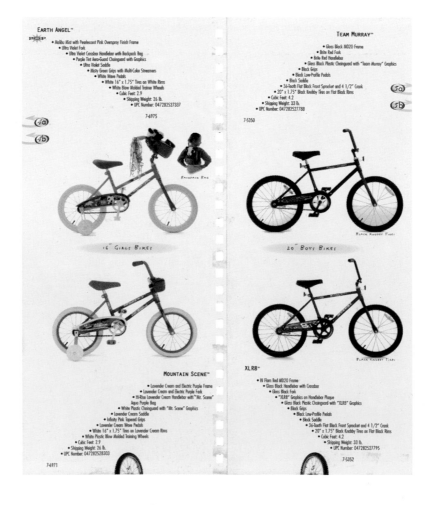

Rock Climber™

- 21-Speed Index Shifting with Black Stripped Casings
- 18" Black Chrome OST Frame with Cable Stops
- Black Chrome OST Fork with End Plugs
- Black Chrome MTB Handlebar
- New Black Finish, Bulge 120 mm Handlebar Stem
- New Chrome-Finish Power Torque Front Sprocket with Black Chain Ring
- Black Brake Levers with Cantilever Brakes
- New Wide Body, Chrome-Finish Front Hub
- New Black Water-Resistant Head Set Cap with Black Head Nut
- New Black MTB Grips
- Black MTB Pedals
- Black MTB Saddle
- Large Black Water Bottle with Dust Cover and Cage
- 26" x 2.0" Black Hammer Tires on Alloy Painted Rims
- Cubic Feet: 6.8
- Shipping Weight: 43 lb.
- UPC Number: 047282528181

7-9692

21-Speed Index Shifting
Mountain Bikes

Rock Climber™

- 21-Speed Index Shifting with Black Stripped Casings
- 18" Black Chrome OST Frame with Cable Stops
- Black Chrome OST Fork with End Plugs
- Black Chrome MTB Handlebar
- New Black Finish, Bulge 120 mm Handlebar Stem
- New Chrome-Finish Power Torque Front Sprocket with Black Chain Ring
- Black Brake Levers with Cantilever Brakes
- New Wide Body, Chrome-Finish Front Hub
- New Black Water-Resistant Head Set Cap with Black Head Nut
- New Black MTB Grips
- Black MTB Saddle
- Large Black Water Bottle with Dust Cover and Cage
- 26" x 2.0" Black Hammer Tires on Alloy Painted Rims
- Cubic Feet: 6.8
- Shipping Weight: 43 lb.
- UPC Number: 047282528006

7-9693

Contour™

- 18" Red Flake Dual Bar, Sleek Contour Frame
- Red Flake ATB Fork
- New Chrome Bio Handlebar
- Chrome Sprocket and Crank
- Red Flake Chainguard
- Flat Black Fenders
- Black Grips
- Black Resin and Kryton Slip-Resistant Pedals
- Black Comfort Saddle with Springs
- 26" x 2.0" Black Low Rolling Resistant White Wall Tires on Chrome Rims
- Cubic Feet: 6.9
- Shipping Weight: 43 lb.
- UPC Number: 047282527870

7-8500

Ladies' model 7-8501
UPC Number: 047282527887

26" Men's/Ladies' Contours

Ladies' model 7-8537
UPC Number: 047282527900

Contour MCS3™

- Three-Speed Grip Shift™ Shifter with Black Casing
- 18" Black Chrome Dual Bar, Sleek Contour Frame with Cable Guide
- Black Chrome ATB Fork
- 4" Rise Black Chrome Handlebar with Black Foam Grips
- Black 80 mm Handlebar Stem
- Three-Speed Internal Hub with Coaster Brake
- Chrome Sprocket and Crank
- Black Chrome Chainguard
- Flat Black Fenders
- Black Resin and Kryton Slip-Resistant Pedals
- Black Comfort Saddle with Springs
- 26" x 2.0" Black Low Rolling Resistant Tires on Chrome Rims
- Cubic Feet: 6.9
- Shipping Weight: 43 lb.
- UPC Number: 047282527894

7-8536

Westport™

- Flam Black Cherry with White Overspray Cantilever Frame
- Flam Black Cherry Fork
- New Chrome Bio Handlebar and Stem with Black Comfort Grips
- Flam Black Cherry Chainguard with "Westport" Graphics
- Painted Fenders with White Pin Stripe
- Coaster Brake
- Black Comfort Saddle with Springs
- 26" x 2.125" Whitewall Tires on Chrome Rims
- Cubic Feet: 7.1
- Shipping Weight: 45 lb.
- UPC Number: 047282527603

7-5032

Ladies' model 7-5033
UPC Number: 047282527597

26" Cruisers

Ladies' model 7-5063
UPC Number: 047282527757

Ocean Breeze™

- 6-Speed Thumb Shifting
- Gloss Black with Silver Overspray Cantilever Frame
- Gloss Black Fork
- New Chrome Bio Handlebar with Black Foam Sleeves and Grips
- Front and Rear Black Side Pull Brakes with Black Casings
- Gloss Black Chainguard with "Ocean Breeze" Graphics
- Black Comfort Saddle with Springs
- 26" x 2.125" Whitewall Tires on Chrome Rims
- Cubic Feet: 7.1
- Shipping Weight: 45 lb.
- UPC Number: 047282527740

7-5062

Zoom. We've got new bikes with knockout features and hot designs.

Whoosh. We've got push-the-envelope ideas that we've incorporated just about everywhere you look.

Zap. We've done more in-depth research than ever before and that helped give us ideas. Sharp, tough, breakthrough ideas.

Ka-boom. Welcome to Murray 1997. Ain't nobody going slow here.

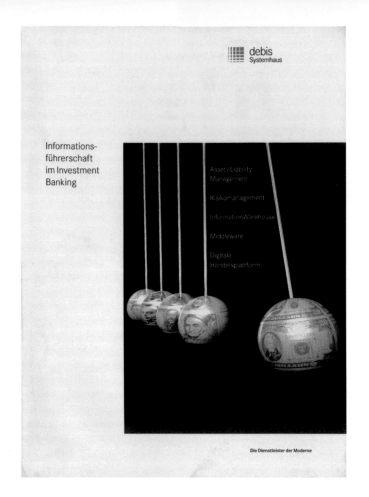

Creative Firm   **Sign Kommunikation GmbH**
                       Frankfurt, Germany
Client   *Debis Systemhaus GmbH*

Inside pages and cover are all printed on the same white matte paper. Back inside cover has a small corner (triangle) pocket. Four-color process in conjunction with metallic inks and varnish were used in the printing of this 8-1/2" x 11-3/4" brochure.

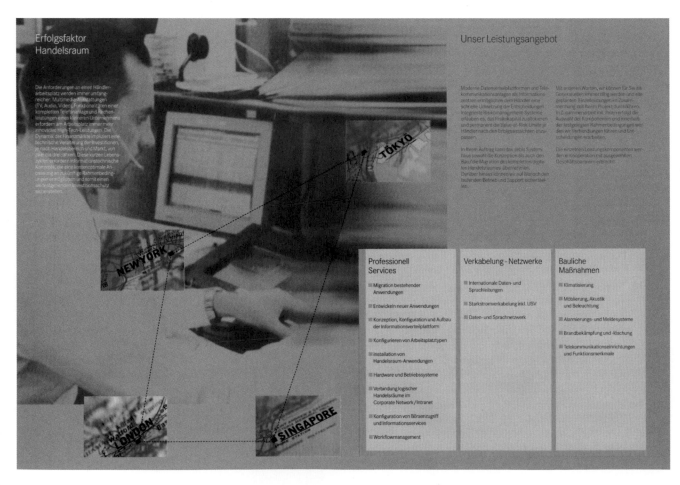

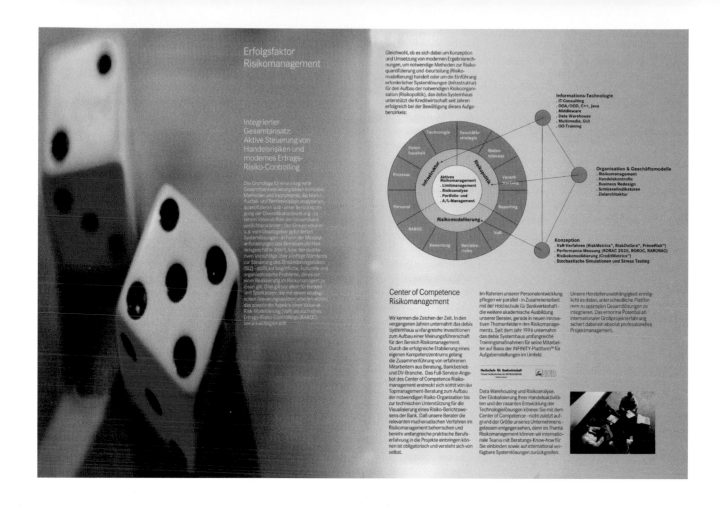

Erfolgsfaktor Risikomanagement

Integrierter Gesamtansatz: Aktive Steuerung von Handelsrisiken und modernes Ertrags-Risiko-Controlling

Die Grundlage für eine integrierte Gesamtbanksteuerung bilden komplexe Methoden und Instrumente, die Markt-, Ausfall- und Betriebsrisiken analysieren, quantifizieren und – unter Berücksichtigung der Diversifikationswirkung – zu einem Value-at-Risk der Gesamtbank verdichten können. Der Einsatz solcher Systemlösungen – in Form der Mindestanforderungen an das Betreiben der Handelsgeschäfte (MaH), bzw. der qualitativen Vorschläge über künftige Standards zur Steuerung des Zinsänderungsrisikos (BIZ) – stößt auf begriffliche, kulturelle und organisatorische Probleme, die es vor einer Realisierung im Risikomanagement zu lösen gilt. Dies gilt vor allem für Banken und Sparkassen, die mit einem strategischen Steuerungssystem arbeiten wollen, das sowohl die Aspekte einer Value-at-Risk-Modellierung (VaR) als auch eines Ertrags-Risiko-Controllings (RAROC) berücksichtigen soll.

Gleichwohl, ob es sich dabei um Konzeption und Umsetzung von modernen Ergebnisrechnungen, um notwendige Methoden zur Risikoquantifizierung und -beurteilung (Risikomodellierung) handelt oder um die Einführung erforderlicher Systemlösungen (Infrastruktur) für den Aufbau der notwendigen Risikoorganisation (Risikopolitik), das debis Systemhaus unterstützt die Kreditwirtschaft seit Jahren erfolgreich bei der Bewältigung dieses Aufgabenzirkels:

Informations-Technologie
. IT-Consulting
. OOA/OOD, C++, Java
. Middleware
. Data Warehouse
. Multimedia, GUI
. OO-Training

Organisation & Geschäftsmodelle
. Risikomanagement
. Handelskontrolle
. Business Redesign
. Schlüsselindikatoren
. Zielarchitektur

Konzeption
. VaR-Verfahren (RiskMetrics™, RiskDollars™, PrimeRisk™)
. Performance-Messung (RORAC 2020, ROROC, RARORAC)
. Risikokonsolidierung (CreditMetrics™)
. Stochastische Simulationen und Stress Testing

Center of Competence Risikomanagement

Wir kennen die Zeichen der Zeit. In den vergangenen Jahren unternahm das debis Systemhaus umfangreiche Investitionen zum Aufbau einer Meinungsführerschaft für den Bereich Risikomanagement. Durch die erfolgreiche Etablierung eines eigenen Kompetenzzentrums gelang die Zusammenführung von erfahrenen Mitarbeitern aus Beratung, Bankbetrieb und DV-Branche. Das Full-Service-Angebot des Center of Competence Risikomanagement erstreckt sich somit von der Topmanagement-Beratung zum Aufbau der notwendigen Risiko-Organisation bis zur technischen Unterstützung für die Visualisierung eines Risiko-Berichtswesens der Bank. Daß unsere Berater die relevanten mathematischen Verfahren im Risikomanagement beherrschen und bereits umfangreiche praktische Berufserfahrung in die Projekte einbringen können ist obligatorisch und versteht sich von selbst.

Im Rahmen unserer Personalentwicklung pflegen wir parallel – in Zusammenarbeit mit der Hochschule für Bankwirtschaft – die weitere akademische Ausbildung unserer Berater, gerade in neuen innovativen Themenfeldern des Risikomanagements. Seit dem Jahr 1996 unternahm das debis Systemhaus umfangreiche Trainingsmaßnahmen für seine Mitarbeiter auf Basis der INFINITY-Plattform™ für Aufgabenstellungen im Umfeld.

Unsere Herstellerunabhängigkeit ermöglicht es dabei, unterschiedliche Plattformen zu optimalen Gesamtlösungen zu integrieren. Das enorme Potential an internationaler Großprojekterfahrung sichert dabei ein absolut professionelles Projektmanagement.

Data Warehousing und Risikoanalyse. Der Globalisierung Ihrer Handelsaktivitäten und der rasanten Entwicklung der Technologielösungen können Sie mit dem Center of Competence – nicht zuletzt aufgrund der Größe unseres Unternehmens – gelassen entgegensehen, denn im Thema Risikomanagement können wir internationale Teams mit Beratungs-Know-how für Sie einbinden sowie auf international verfügbare Systemlösungen zurückgreifen.

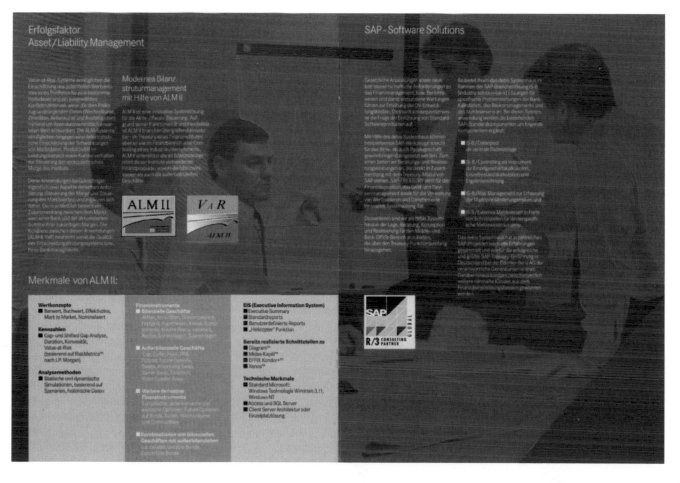

Erfolgsfaktor Asset/Liability Management

Modernes Bilanzstrukturmanagement mit Hilfe von ALM II

Value-at-Risk-Systeme ermöglichen die Einschätzung des potentiellen Wertverlustes eines Portfolios für eine bestimmte Haltedauer und ein ausgewähltes Konfidenzintervall, wenn die dem Risiko zugrundeliegenden Daten (Wechselkurse, Zinssätze, Aktienkurse) und Ausfallrisiken innerhalb um ihren durchschnittlichen erwarteten Wert schwanken. Die ALM-Systeme ermöglichen hingegen eine deterministische Einschätzung der Schwankungen von Marktdaten, Produktivität im Leistungsbereich sowie Kundenverhalten zur Sicherung der vorausgezeichneten Marge des Institutes.

Merkmale von ALM II:

Wertkonzepte
■ Barwert, Buchwert, Effektivzins, Mark to Market, Nominalwert

Kennzahlen
■ Gap- und Shifted Gap Analyse, Duration, Konvexität, Value-at-Risk (basierend auf RiskMetrics™ nach J.P. Morgan)

Analysemethoden
■ Statische und dynamische Simulationen, basierend auf Szenarien, historische Daten

Finanzinstrumente
■ Bilanzielle Geschäfte
Aktiva, Annuitäten, Diskontpapiere, Festgeld, Hypotheken, Kredite, Kontokorrente, Kredite (fest u. variabel), Roll-over-Schichtungen, Sparanlagen

■ Außerbilanzielle Geschäfte
Cap, Collar, Floor, FRA, Futures, Future-Optionen, Swaps, Amortising Swaps, Basis-Swaps, Forward-Swaps, Roller Coaster Swaps

■ Weitere derivative Finanzinstrumente
Europäische, amerikanische und exotische Optionen, Future-Optionen auf Bonds, Aktien, Wechselkurse und Commodities

■ Kombinationen von bilanziellen Geschäften mit außerbilanziellen Geschäften
u.a. Callable Yield Curve Bonds, Convertible Bonds

EIS (Executive Information System)
■ Executive Summary
■ Standardreports
■ Benutzerdefinierte Reports
■ „Helicopter" Funktion

Bereits realisierte Schnittstellen zu
■ Diagram™
■ Midas-Kapiti™
■ EFFIX Kondor+™
■ Xenos™

Technische Merkmale
■ Standard Microsoft: Windows Technologie Windows 3.11, Windows NT
■ Access und SQL Server
■ Client Server Architektur oder Einzelplatzlösung

SAP - Software Solutions

Gesetzliche Anpassungen schaffen neue betriebswirtschaftliche Anforderungen an das Finanzmanagement bzw. Berichtswesen und damit verbundene Wartungsaufwendungen für Einführung und DV-Entwicklungskosten. Daher sollten konsequenterweise die Frage der Einführung von Standard-Softwareprodukten aufkommen.

Mit Hilfe des debis Systemhaus können beispielsweise SAP-Werkzeuge sowohl für das Aktiv- als auch Passivgeschäft gewinnbringend eingesetzt werden. Zum einen bieten wir Beratungs- und Realisierungsleistungen an, die direkt in Zusammenhang mit dem Treasury-Modul von SAP stehen, SAP-TREASURY wird für die Finanzdisposition, das Geld- und Devisenmanagement sowie für die Verwaltung von Wertpapieren und Darlehen eingesetzt.

Da wir darüber hinaus das debis Systemhaus in der Lage, Beratung, Konzeption und Realisierung für den Middle- und Back-Office-Bereich anzubieten, die über den Treasury-Funktionsumfang hinausgehen.

Sie bietet Ihnen das debis Systemhaus im Rahmen der SAP-Branchenlösung IS-B (Industry solution-bank) Lösungen für spezifische Problemstellungen der Bankkalkulation, des Risikomanagements und des Meldewesens an. Bei dieser Systemanwendung werden die bestehenden SAP-Standardkomponenten um folgende Komponenten ergänzt:

■ IS-B/Datenpool
als zentrale Datenträger

■ IS-B/Controlling als Instrument zur Einzelgeschäftskalkulation, Einzelbestandskalkulation und Ergebnisrechnung

■ IS-B/Risk Management zur Erfassung der Marktrisikomessung und

■ IS-B/Externes Meldewesen in Form von Schnittstellen für länderspezifische Meldewesen

Das debis Systemhaus hat in jahrelangen SAP-Projekten wertvolle Erfahrungen gesammelt und war für die erfolgreiche und größte SAP-Treasury Einführung in Deutschland bei der Daimler-Benz AG der verantwortliche Generalunternehmer.

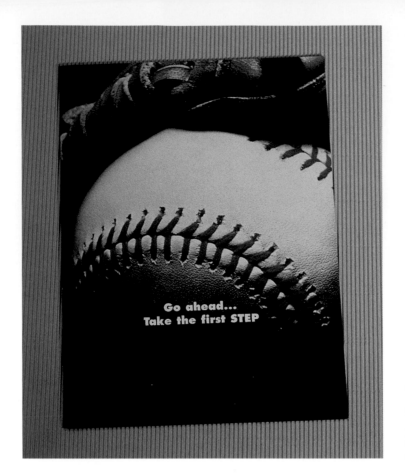

Creative Firm   **Cantor Design Assoc. Inc.**
New York, New York

Client   *New York Life Insurance Company*

Brochure cover and interior were both printed on
the same heavy weight of white matte paper:
8-3/4" x 11-3/4".

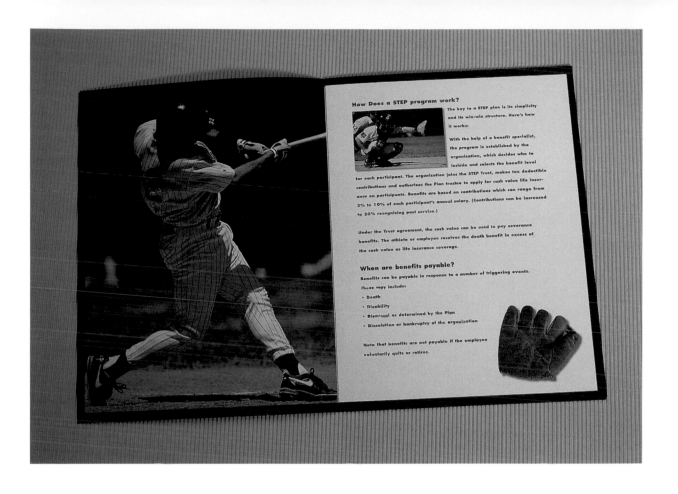

How Does a STEP program work?

The key to a STEP plan is its simplicity and its win-win structure. Here's how it works:

With the help of a benefit specialist, the program is established by the organization, which decides who to include and selects the benefit level for each participant. The organization joins the STEP Trust, makes tax deductible contributions and authorizes the Plan trustee to apply for cash value life insurance on participants. Benefits are based on contributions which can range from 2% to 10% of each participant's annual salary. (Contributions can be increased to 20% recognizing past service.)

Under the Trust agreement, the cash value can be used to pay severance benefits. The athlete or employee receives the death benefit in excess of the cash value as life insurance coverage.

When are benefits payable?

Benefits can be payable in response to a number of triggering events. These may include:

- Death
- Disability
- Dismissal as determined by the Plan
- Dissolution or bankruptcy of the organization

Note that benefits are not payable if the employee voluntarily quits or retires.

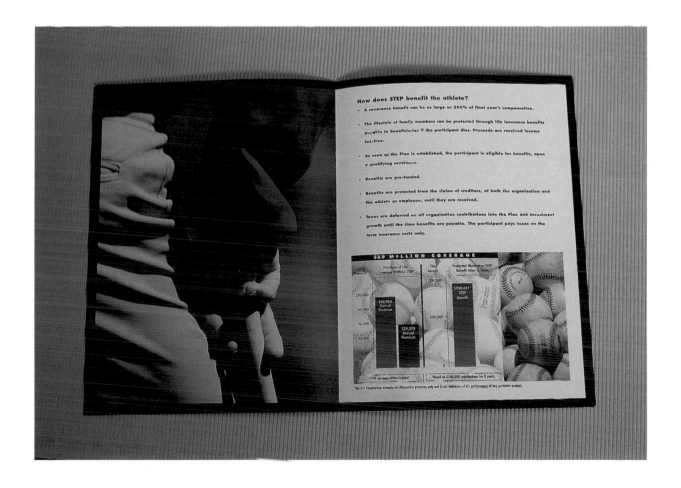

How does STEP benefit the athlete?

- A severance benefit can be as large as 200% of final year's compensation.

- The lifestyle of family members can be protected through life insurance benefits payable to beneficiaries if the participant dies. Proceeds are received income tax-free.

- As soon as the Plan is established, the participant is eligible for benefits, upon a qualifying severance.

- Benefits are pre-funded.

- Benefits are protected from the claims of creditors, of both the organization and the athlete or employee, until they are received.

- Taxes are deferred on all organization contributions into the Plan and investment growth until the time benefits are payable. The participant pays taxes on the term insurance costs only.

Creative Firm   **Allan Burrows Limited**
                    Ingatestone, England
Client   *Ford Motor Company Limited*

Cover is completely wrapped in printed vellum. Four-color printing and varnish are used on cream, glossy stock in this 8-1/4" x 11-5/8" brochure.

Your life

No in-tray, no meetings, no phones. It's time to relax and unwind. Take stock and recharge your batteries. Feel the wind in your hair, watch a spectacular sunset or enjoy an intimate meal at your favourite restaurant. After all, you work to live not live to work.

Optional leather trim shown.

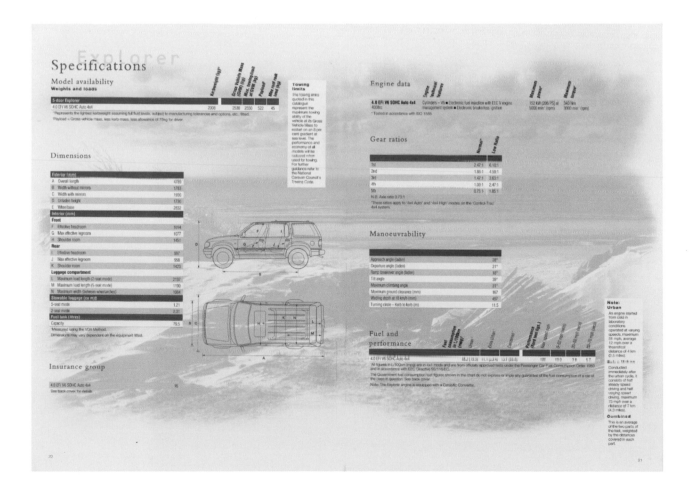

Explorer

Specifications

Model availability
Weights and loads

5-door Explorer	Kerbweight (kg)*	Gross Vehicle Mass (GVM) (kg)	Max. towing load at GVM (kg)	Payload*	Max roof rack load (kg)
4.0 EFI V6 SOHC Auto 4x4	2008	2530	2550	522	45

*Represents the lightest kerbweight assuming full fuel levels, subject to manufacturing tolerances and options, etc. fitted.
*Payload = Gross vehicle mass, less kerb mass, less allowance of 75kg for driver.

Dimensions

Exterior (mm)	
A Overall length	4780
B Width without mirrors	1783
C Width with mirrors	1956
D Unladen height	1730
E Wheelbase	2832
Interior (mm)	
Front	
F Effective headroom	1014
G Max effective legroom	1077
H Shoulder room	1451
Rear	
I Effective headroom	997
J Max effective legroom	958
K Shoulder room	1423
Luggage compartment	
L Maximum load length (2-seat mode)	2137
M Maximum load length (5-seat mode)	1190
N Maximum width (between wheelarches)	1064
Stowable luggage (cu m)‡	
5-seat mode	1.21
2-seat mode	2.31
Fuel tank (litres)	
Capacity	79.5

‡Measured using the VDA Method.
Dimensions may vary depending on the equipment fitted.

Insurance group

4.0 EFI V6 SOHC Auto 4x4	16

See back cover for details.

Towing limits

The towing limits quoted in this catalogue represent the maximum towing ability of the vehicle at its Gross Vehicle Mass to restart on an 8 per cent gradient at sea level. The performance and economy of all models will be reduced when used for towing. For further guidance refer to the National Caravan Council's Towing Code.

Engine data

4.0 EFI V6 SOHC Auto 4x4	Engine technical features	Maximum power*	Maximum torque*
4.0 EFI V6 SOHC Auto 4x4	Cylinders – V6 ■ Electronic fuel injection with EEC V engine management system ■ Electronic breakerless ignition	152 kW (205 PS) at 5000 min⁻¹ (rpm)	345 Nm 3000 min⁻¹ (rpm)
4086cc			

* Tested in accordance with ISO 1585.

Gear ratios

	Normal*	Low Ratio
1st	2.47:1	6.10:1
2nd	1.86:1	4.59:1
3rd	1.47:1	3.63:1
4th	1.00:1	2.47:1
5th	0.75:1	1.85:1

N.B. Axle ratio 3.73:1
*These ratios apply to '4x4 Auto' and '4x4 High' modes on the 'Control-Trac' 4x4 system.

Manoeuvrability

Approach angle (laden)	28°
Departure angle (laden)	21°
Ramp breakover angle (laden)	16°
Tilt angle	35°
Maximum climbing angle	31°
Maximum ground clearance (mm)	167
Wading depth at 10 km/h (mm)	457
Turning circle - Kerb to kerb (m)	11.5

Fuel and performance

4.0 EFI V6 SOHC Auto 4x4	Fuel consumption in l/100km (mpg)			Performance (figures quoted approx.)		
	Urban	Extra Urban	Combined	Max. speed mph	0-60 mph (secs)	30-70 mph (secs)
4.0 EFI V6 SOHC Auto 4x4	18.2 (15.5)	11.1 (21.4)	13.7 (20.6)	106	10.0	9.7

The figures in l/100km (mpg) are in 4x4 mode and are from officially approved tests under the Passenger Car Fuel Consumption Order 1983 and in accordance with EEC Directive 93/116/EC.
The Government fuel consumption test figures shown in the chart do not express or imply any guarantee of the fuel consumption of a car of this class in question. See back cover.
Note: The Explorer engine is equipped with a Catalytic Converter.

Note:

Urban
An engine started from cold in laboratory conditions operated at varying speeds, maximum 31 mph, average 12 mph over a theoretical distance of 4 km (2.5 miles).

Extra Urban
Conducted immediately after the urban cycle. It consists of half steady speed driving and half varying speed driving, maximum 75 mph over a distance of 7 km (4.3 miles).

Combined
This is an average of the two parts of the test, weighted by the distances covered in each part.

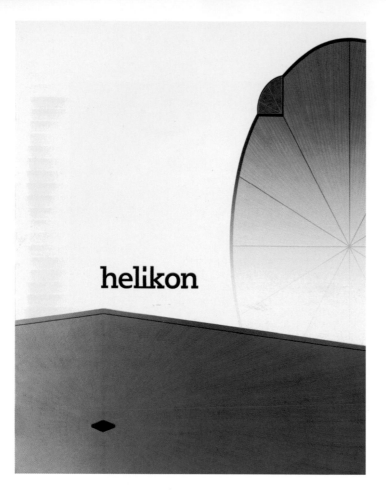

helikon

Creative Firm   **Jones Studio Limited**
                 Staten Island, New York
Client   *Helikon Furniture Company*

Interesting photographic effects are printed on white semigloss paper.
Bound with extending staples (for easy storage in a notebook) this brochure
is 8-1/2" x 11".

Conference table of highly figured
eucalyptus, white oak and black
inlay. Top and base are finely
finished with 2.25" thick fluted edge
detail carved from solid white oak.
w 144" d 58/38" h 29"
Chairs: Kita 1414N

conferencing in style

Helikon's skillfulness is witnessed
in the fabrication of elaborate table
designs. From concept to finished
product, a close dialogue is
maintained between our engineers
and the specifier. Construction
drawings are always submitted for
client approval before custom
work begins.

There are few limits to the variety
and combination of materials that
may be specified – stone, laminate,
leather, metal and wood are most
popular. A complex superstructure
is developed for each table
designed to reinforce tops, prevent
bowing and maintain a tighter fit at
all joints. It is this kind of attention
to quality and detail that has gained
Helikon a reputation for design
excellence which is recognized
worldwide.

Stonington desk in mahogany
solids and flat-cut veneer.
w 72" d 36" h 29.5"

Stonington round conference table
with mahogany finish.
ø 48" h 29.5"

Understated elegance and
authentic detailing define the
Stonington Collection. Designed by
Peter Wooding, after extensive
research into 18th and 19th
century American furniture design,
Stonington offers a skillful blend of
traditional design with state of the
art features to accommodate the
needs of today's office.

Custom Stonington L-shaped
configuration composed of single
pedestal desk, bridge, CRT corner
and credenza/junction unit with
glass door. Grommets, wire chases,
nets, and other wire management
features are incorporated in the
unit, as well as printer shelf and
other electronic storage.
Desk: w 78" d 36" h 29.5"
Chair: Dillon 1209

Custom L-shaped reception desk in
makore, pomele makore, mahogany
solids with ebonized inlay, quirk
detail, and white granite.
w 96" d 84" h 42"

Custom U-shaped reception desk in
makore, pomele makore, mahogany
solids with ebonized inlay, quirk
detail, and Andes black granite.
w 96" d 84" h 42"

Helikon offers a wide range of
custom capabilities for caseguods
manufacturing, from the
line-specific, which incorporate
detailing from our standard
product series, to completely
custom, based on a clients
requirements. A design is not
limited to fine hardwoods and
veneers - granite, marble, plastic
laminate, and manufactured
state-of-the-art materials are
often specified.

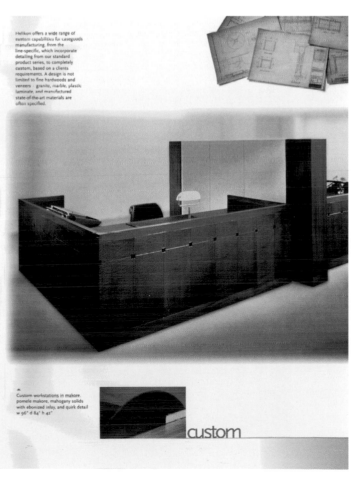

Custom workstations in makore,
pomele makore, mahogany solids
with ebonized inlay, and quirk detail
w 96" d 84" h 42"

custom

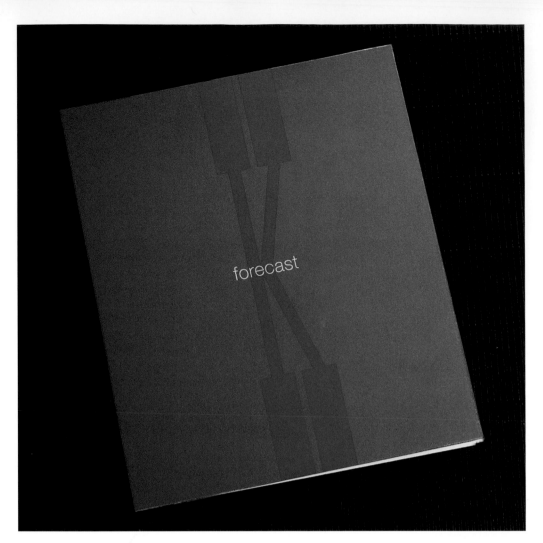

forecast

Creative Firm **2x4**
New York,
New York
Client *Knoll Inc.*

Spiral-bound brochure has
many fold-out pages. Black
cover is included in binding,
but brochure jacket is not. All
printing is done on white
matte stock. Size is 6-3/4" x 8".

The solution to one problem
may be the origin of another.

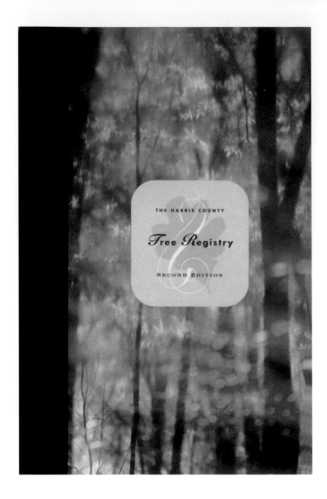

Creative Firm   **Savage Design Group**
                      Houston, Texas
Client   *The Park People, Inc.*

Glued binding holds together 5-7/8" x 9" brochure. White
matte stocks (Coronado SST Recycled 80 lb. cover and 50 lb.
cover) are contrasted by beautiful handmade endpapers
which include actual leaves and leaf parts.

index

Determining a champion tree.

$Circumference^{(in)} + Height^{(ft)} + 1/4\ Spread^{(ft)} = Index$

{ 2 -- -- 3 } *The biggest indexes are the champions!*

What is a tree?

A tree is a woody plant with an erect perennial trunk at least 3"
in diameter, a definitely formed crown of foliage, and a height
of at least 13'. In contrast, a shrub is a small woody plant usually
having several perennial stems branching from the base.

Crapemyrtle, Common (*Lagerstroemia indica*)

David Pace, 707 Omar, Houston

| Circumference: 116" | Height: 38' | Spread: 36' | INDEX: 163 |

Devil's Walkingstick (*Aralia spinosa*)

City of Houston, Arboretum & Nature Center

| Circumference: 10' | Height: 18' | Spread: 5' | INDEX: 29 |

Dogwood, Flowering (*Cornus florida*)

A.E. Strother, 206 E. Sunnyside, Houston

| Circumference: 47" | Height: 24' | Spread: 36' | INDEX: 80 |

Elm, American (*Ulmus americana*)

Bayou Bend Collection, No. 1 Westcott, Houston

| Circumference: 152" | Height: 117' | Spread: 80' | INDEX: 289 |

Elm, Chinese (*Parvi folia*)

City of Houston, Cullinan Park, 6700 Long Drive

| Circumference: 114" | Height: 57' | Spread: 68' | INDEX: 188 |

Elm, Water (*Planera aquatica*)

Harris County Precinct 4, Burroughs Park, Houston

| Circumference: 61" | Height: 40' | Spread: 41' | INDEX: 111 |

Elm, Winged (*Ulmus alata*)

Harris County Precinct 4, Burroughs Park, Houston

| Circumference: 105" | Height: 70' | Spread: 96' | INDEX: 199 |

Ginkgo (*Ginkgo biloba*)

Harris County Precinct 4, Burroughs Park, Houston

| Circumference: 17" | Height: 32' | Spread: 96' | INDEX: 54 |

American Elm

{ 6 -- -- 7 }

A woodland in full color is awesome
as a forest fire, in magnitude at least:
but a single tree is like a dancing
tongue of flame to warm the heart.

—Hal Borland

89

The "Cemetery Oak" located at the far south end of Glenwood Cemetery is a truly magnificent Live Oak specimen that stands as guardian over the deceased beneath its massive span.

Post Oak

City of Baytown, Texas Avenue at Highway 146			
Circumference: 188"	Height: 57'	Spread: 68'	INDEX: 262
Joel & Lynne Gevirtz, 3611 Audubon, Houston			
Circumference: 173"	Height: 64'	Spread: 100'	INDEX: 262
John & Marjorie Freeman, 4404 Mount Vernon, Houston			
Circumference: 160"	Height: 76'	Spread: 102'	INDEX: 256
(owner unknown), 2900 Crawford, Houston			
Circumference: 178"	Height: 55'	Spread: 93'	INDEX: 256
Magnificat House, 3200 Caroline, Houston			
Circumference: 193"	Height: 40'	Spread: 78'	INDEX: 252
Alma Mowery, FM 1960 Area, Houston			
Circumference: 163"	Height: 61'	Spread: 92'	INDEX: 247
"Old Hanging Oak," City of Houston, 600 Bagby			
Circumference: 178"	Height: 45'	Spread: 97'	INDEX: 247
Judy Evans, 14514 Broadgreen, Houston			
Circumference: 166"	Height: 53'	Spread: 91'	INDEX: 242
Riecke Baumann, 2404 Pelham, Houston			
Circumference: 153"	Height: 62'	Spread: 110'	INDEX: 242
Ruby Andrews, 1112 Jerome, Houston			
Circumference: 154"	Height: 70'	Spread: 69'	INDEX: 241
Glenwood Cemetery, 2525 Washington Ave., Houston			
Circumference: 156"	Height: 60'	Spread: 94'	INDEX: 240
Oak Place C.I.A., 3110 Evergreen, Houston			
Circumference: 163"	Height: 52'	Spread: 96'	INDEX: 239
Marsha Green, 10318 Mayfield Road, Houston			
Circumference: 163"	Height: 55'	Spread: 80'	INDEX: 238

Michelle & Hector Herrera, 2233 Chilton Rd., Houston

| Circumference: 155" | Height: 59' | Spread: 94' | INDEX: 238 |

David Lake, 209 Teetshorn, Houston

| Circumference: 148" | Height: 63' | Spread: 93' | INDEX: 234 |

Gary & Linda Tatum, 6309 Rodrigo, Houston

| Circumference: 146" | Height: 62' | Spread: 87' | INDEX: 230 |

Ray & Peggy Mitchell, 3009 Avalon, Houston

| Circumference: 150" | Height: 56' | Spread: 96' | INDEX: 230 |

The Johnsons, 1814 Sunset Blvd., Houston

| Circumference: 148" | Height: 59' | Spread: 90' | INDEX: 230 |

*N*o town can fail of beauty, though its walks were gutters and its houses hovels, if venerable trees make magnificent colonnades along its streets. *—Henry Ward Beecher*

Houston Parks Board, 2999 South Wayside

| Circumference: 111" | Height: 96' | Spread: 84' | INDEX: 228 |

Jo Ann Matthiesen, 2345 Glen Haven Blvd., Houston

| Circumference: 129" | Height: 72' | Spread: 103' | INDEX: 227 |

Martha Turner Properties, 1902 Westheimer, Houston

| Circumference: 145" | Height: 59' | Spread: 87' | INDEX: 226 |

St. Peter United Church of Christ, 9022 Long Point, Houston

| Circumference: 146" | Height: 58' | Spread: 90' | INDEX: 226 |

Oak, Post *(Quercus stellata)*

Mark & Linda Gonzales, 835 Rutland, Houston

| Circumference: 113" | Height: 55' | Spread: 81' | INDEX: 188 |

Annie Skyvara, 821 Oxford, Houston

| Circumference: 125" | Height: 78' | Spread: 69' | INDEX: 220 |

Alice Sigurdson & Sandy Frank, 927 Redan, Houston

| Circumference: 117" | Height: 83' | Spread: 71' | INDEX: 218 |

Karen & Mike Matthews, 801 Merrill, Houston

| Circumference: 120" | Height: 75' | Spread: 60' | INDEX: 210 |

Margaret Sparks, 910 Byrne, Houston

| Circumference: 128" | Height: 65' | Spread: 64' | INDEX: 209 |

Martin Kopacz, 948 Redan, Houston

| Circumference: 124" | Height: 72' | Spread: 50' | INDEX: 208 |

Randall J. Gross, 11830 Chapelwood Lane, Houston

| Circumference: 137" | Height: 49' | Spread: 62' | INDEX: 202 |

Faith Venverloh, 428 Westmoreland, Houston

| Circumference: 122" | Height: 61' | Spread: 68' | INDEX: 200 |

Parasol, Chinese *(Firmiana simplex)*

Gold Lance Corporation, 1920 North Memorial Way

| Circumference: 40" | Height: 17' | Spread: 22' | INDEX: 62 |

Pecan *(Carya illinoensis)*

Gerard Brown, 902 Merrill, Houston

| Circumference: 139" | Height: 82' | Spread: 76' | INDEX: 240 |

Sally Quast, 4400 Kyle, Houston

| Circumference: 140" | Height: 78' | Spread: 75' | INDEX: 237 |

John & Wende Bos, 1101 Legreen, Houston

| Circumference: 131" | Height: 80' | Spread: 84' | INDEX: 232 |

Phillip & Kelley McCollough, 807 W. Cottage, Houston

| Circumference: 118" | Height: 90' | Spread: 73' | INDEX: 226 |

Chinese Parasol

91

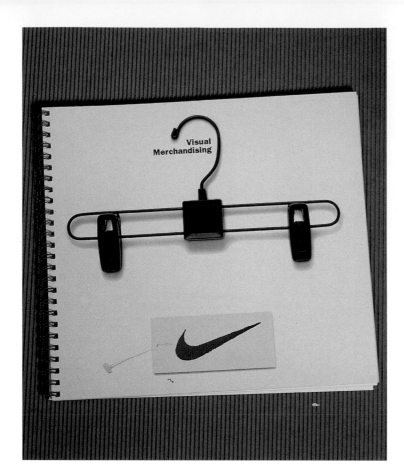

Creative Firm   **Matite Giovanotte**
                  Forli, Italy
Client   *Nike Italy*

White and cream matte papers are the base for this 9-1/2" x 8-3/4"
brochure. Red spiral binding is used. Inside, one of the pages folds
out while several others are graced with printed vellum overlays.

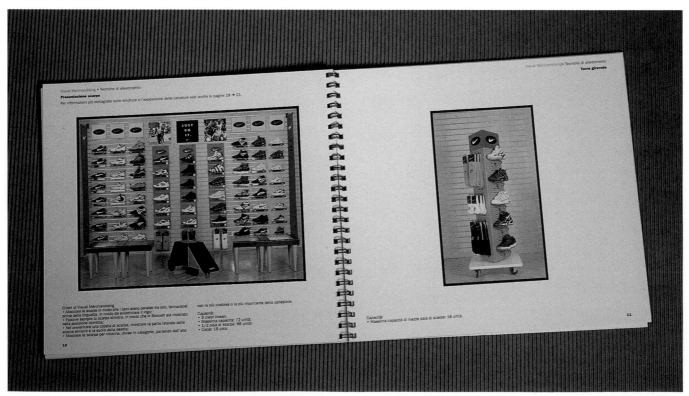

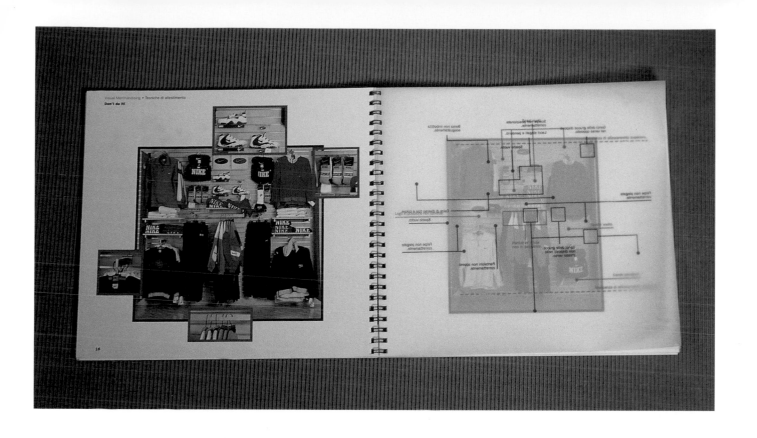

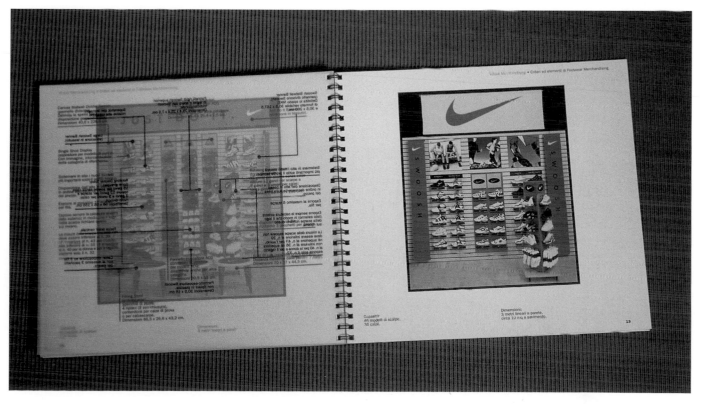

Product Portfolio

Jafra
Cosmetics International

Creative Firm   **Wiley Designs**
              Westlake Village, California
Client   *Jafra Cosmetics International*

Nearly square, 7-1/4" x 7 1/8", brochure uses text weight semigloss white paper for cover and inside pages.

Skin Care as Individual as You

Four advanced Skin Care systems developed to meet your individual needs. Each state-of-the-art product, when used as part of a complete system, helps to regulate and balance your unique skin toward its normal or "ideal" state. Each system puts today's latest, most scientifically advanced technology, to work for you. All products are clinically, allergy, irritancy, and dermatologist tested.

Replenish System--
for dry skin
If you've noticed a dry, taut feeling, fine lines or loss of elasticity and resiliency, Replenish System formula will go to work for you. Products used together in this system incorporate the most advanced vitamin-derived ingredients and long-term liposome moisture delivery system to hydrate your dry skin and to help diminish the appearance of fine lines.

Refining System--
for dry to normal skin
If you experience occasional breakouts or dry patches on your otherwise smooth, even-textured, evenly colored skin, the light yet emollient-rich formulas in this system are for you. All Refining System products work together to provide the light moisturization and conditioning benefits that will help restore dehydrated areas of the skin.

Balance System--
for normal to oily skin
If certain areas of your skin look and feel dry while others occasionally show signs of oily breakthrough, particularly in the T-zone area of forehead/nose/chin, you will benefit from a system capable of treating and balancing both conditions. These formulas offer bio-technological ingredients to adjust partly oily combination skin with sebum oil control and moisture delivery, as needed. In the process, they help smooth skin by minimizing the appearance of larger pores.

Control System--
for oily skin
If your skin has an oily shine, enlarged pores, or is subject to blemishes and dullness, you should benefit from the Control System. This system helps to regulate and balance skin toward a more normal state--even helping to minimize the appearance of large pores and to reduce blemishes. Control System products work toward absorbing excess oils without stripping skin.

Jafra Skin Programmer
Which skin type best describes yours? Our unique electronic analysis machine will scientifically determine your skin type, and hence, your skin's needs by accurately measuring the degree of moisture in the upper layers of your skin. Ask your participating Jafra Consultant for your own analysis.

The Art of Soft, Subtle Color

Behind this beautiful face is the Jafra collection of foundation, color and makeup. Jafra puts the means to a beautiful, flawless face at your fingertips. Here is everything you need to contour and highlight your best assets, to capitalize on your uniqueness and to make the most of the classic and fashion hues that work for you.

Applying Foundation

Start with a scrupulously clean and moisturized face using your personal Jafra Skin Care System. Apply foundation to the entire face and neck area, using gentle, upward and outward strokes to keep from clogging pores.

Foundation

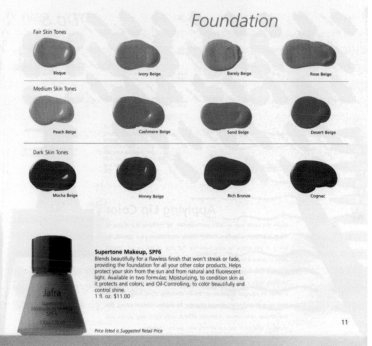

Fair Skin Tones: Bisque, Ivory Beige, Barely Beige, Rose Beige

Medium Skin Tones: Peach Beige, Cashmere Beige, Sand Beige, Desert Beige

Dark Skin Tones: Mocha Beige, Honey Beige, Rich Bronze, Cognac

Supertone Makeup, SPF6
Blends beautifully for a flawless finish that won't streak or fade, providing the foundation for all your other color products. Helps protect your skin from the sun and from natural and fluorescent light. Available in two formulas: Moisturizing, to condition skin as it protects and colors; and Oil-Controlling, to color beautifully and control shine.
1 fl. oz. $11.00

Price listed is Suggested Retail Price

10   11

Apricot Cream, Fiesta Fire, Cherry, Clove, Passion Fruit, Grape, Orange, Ginger
Currant, Cinnamon, Pink on Ice, Siren Red, Berry Mist, Copper Frost, Olé, Tropical Red
Pink Frost, Deep Rose, Nutmeg, Plumrose, Wild Rose, Watermelon, Ripe Mango, Bronze
Champagne Frost, Black Raspberry, Red Kerlin, Hot Chocolate, Rose Petal, Berry Frost, Russet
New Olé, Raspberry Wine, Sunswept Coral, Glazed Wine, Shocking Fuchsia, Nude Pink

Lip &

Lasting Lip Color
Luscious color for long-lasting wear. Color stays in place for hours. Feels creamy, not dry.
.12 oz. $7.50

Moisturizing Lipstick, SPF6
Captivating colors combine with silky conditioners to help protect lips from the sun.
.12 oz. $7.50

Applying Lip Color

Begin the same way as Jafra professionals, by defining the shape of the mouth with a lip pencil color closely matched to your lipstick. By filling in the entire lip area with the flat side of the pencil, lipstick stays in place even longer. For more precise results, particularly with stronger colors, apply lipstick with a lip brush. Applying two coats, blotting with a tissue in-between, also increases staying power and creates an opaque appearance. When choosing color, keep in mind that neutral eye colors balance stronger lip shades. Vibrant colors, like the strong reds, create dramatic effects with light skin tones and makeup, and more natural effects with darker coloring.

Nail Color

Watermelon, Coral, Fuchsia, Ripe Mango, Rose Petal, Bronze, Olé
Pure Linen, Satin Red, Champagne Beige, Siren Red, Muslin, Pink On Ice, Raw Silk
Copper Frost, Misty Mauve, Currant, Berry Mist, Russet, Deep Rose, Orange

Nail Lacquer
Jafra formaldehyde-free lacquers coordinate with lipsticks and blushes. Chip and peel resistant, they glide on smoothly and dry to a lustrous brilliance.
.4 fl. oz. $6.50

Date, Coral, Russet, Red, Pomegranate, Rose, Mexican Rose, Burgundy, Fig, Cherry, Cinnamon

Lip Pencils
Soft-textured Jafra pencils enhance lip shape, define lip lines and help prevent lipstick from bleeding and feathering. Colors blend with Jafra lipsticks.
.04 oz. $7.25

All prices listed are Suggested Resale Prices

12   13

Lafayette College

A *R*eport from
Arthur J. Rothkopf, President

December 1996

Creative Firm **Disegno**
Mentor, Ohio
Client *Lafayette College*

Metallic inks, in addition to four-color process printing, are used on this 7" x 10" brochure's white, semigloss cover and interior.

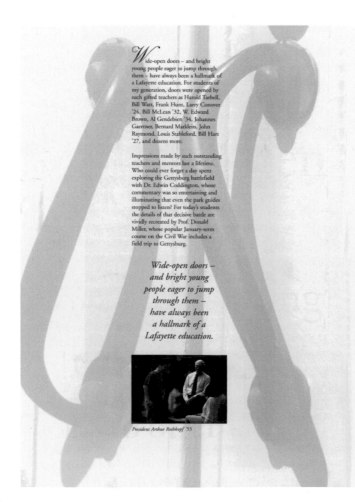

*W*ide-open doors – and bright young people eager to jump through them – have always been a hallmark of a Lafayette education. For students of my generation, doors were opened by such gifted teachers as Harold Tarbell, Bill Watt, Frank Hunt, Larry Conover '24, Bill McLean '32, W. Edward Brown, Al Gendebien '34, Johannes Gaertner, Bernard Marklein, John Raymond, Louis Stableford, Bill Hart '27, and dozens more.

Impressions made by such outstanding teachers and mentors last a lifetime. Who could ever forget a day spent exploring the Gettysburg battlefield with Dr. Edwin Coddington, whose commentary was so entertaining and illuminating that even the park guides stopped to listen? For today's students the details of that decisive battle are vividly recreated by Prof. Donald Miller, whose popular January-term course on the Civil War includes a field trip to Gettysburg.

Wide-open doors – and bright young people eager to jump through them – have always been a hallmark of a Lafayette education.

President Arthur Rothkopf '55

*T*he faculty who unlock these special doors for students do so with a dynamic blend of knowledge, energy, commitment, and imagination. "I am left in no doubt as to what my primary responsibility is at Lafayette," notes Stephen Kaprielian, Assistant Professor of Electrical Engineering; "I am first and foremost a teacher." In recognition of the distinctive and inspiring teaching that occurs at Lafayette, trustee Walter Scott '59 and his wife Kate, endowed the Marquis Distinguished Teaching Awards. Sustained applause greeted the announcement of the award and the recognition of the first four recipients at the trustee-faculty dinner in May.

Students recognize – and celebrate – the benefits of attending a small residential college with remarkable teachers and an enviable 11:1 student/faculty ratio. Josh Narva '96 spoke for many of his peers in acknowledging that faculty had helped him "not because they felt contractually obligated, but because they had a genuine interest in my success both as a student and as a person." In her farewell column as co-editor of *The Lafayette*, Kristine Zeigler '96 summed up her four undergraduate years with heartfelt gratitude: "If I had gone [to the University of California at Berkeley], I would have been an anonymous presence. Instead I became brassy, sassy, outspoken, and far more creative than I ever imagined. Thank you, Lafayette professors, for letting me. I'll always love you for it."

Joshua Narva '96 (right) wrote his honors thesis on the Israeli right wing group, Gush Emunium, and was advised by Ilan Peleg, Charles A. Dana Professor of Government and Law and head of the department.

A faculty as dedicated as Lafayette's makes serious its responsibility for regularly updating and invigorating the curriculum. A good example is the new introductory engineering course offered for the first time last fall. This innovative class divides first-semester engineering students into small teams and challenges them to solve design problems based on an engineering theme. The special resources available to team members last October as they tackled space-shuttle design included shuttle astronaut Col. James Voss, who visited the campus to lecture and meet with ES101 students only a few weeks after he had walked in space as a crew member aboard the Endeavor.

The traditional hour-long lecture attended by rows of students quietly listening to a "sage on the stage" is nearly as obsolete as the slide rule. Increasingly, our faculty serve as coaches and guides, engaging students as active learners and challenging them to take responsibility for their success. Some of the most exhilarating learning occurs outside the typical classroom or course-related lab setting. Mechanical engineering major Scott Billington '96 found his one-to-one research partnerships with faculty to be "more of an education than any class could ever be." These opportunities are truly the gemstones of the engineering program and my experience at Lafayette."

A traditional hour-long lecture attended by rows quietly listening to a "sage on the stage" is nearly as OBSOLETE as the slide rule.

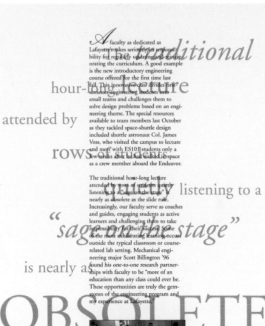

Four weeks after he conducted a six-hour walk in space from the Endeavor Space Shuttle, Col. James Voss was at Lafayette consulting with first-year engineering students about projects they were designing based on a space shuttle theme.

Hogg Hall

Built 1902

While problem-solving exercises undertaken in real-world settings provide excellent preparation for life after graduation, decisions about post-graduate study and career paths require far more thought and exploration than a single course can provide. During the past year, the Office of Career Services put the finishing touches on a comprehensive career-planning program designed to engage and guide each student throughout his or her four years. A donor generously added $1 million to the endowment to support GATEWAY and related initiatives. Although many high-tech features are incorporated, this exciting new program by no means overlooks the importance of direct person-to-person contact. Alumni and alumnae serve as mentors to students and, along with members of the staff, assist in obtaining externships, internships, and summer employment.

Teleconferencing technology is transforming the way students seek jobs – and the way they acquire knowledge. A $550,000 grant secured jointly by Lafayette and Lehigh from the Andrew W. Mellon Foundation is enabling our two institutions to share teaching resources in innovative ways. A course taught by a faculty member in a specially equipped classroom at one institution can be taken interactively by students at the other campus. These cooperative arrangements are particularly beneficial for teaching courses that attract small enrollments or that require highly specialized faculty expertise. The proximity of Lafayette and Lehigh is an added plus; faculty members can move easily from campus to campus during the semester to provide direct personal contact with the students at each site.

Teleconferencing TECHNOLOGY is transforming the way students seek JOBS – and the way they acquire KNOWLEDGE.

Farinon College Center

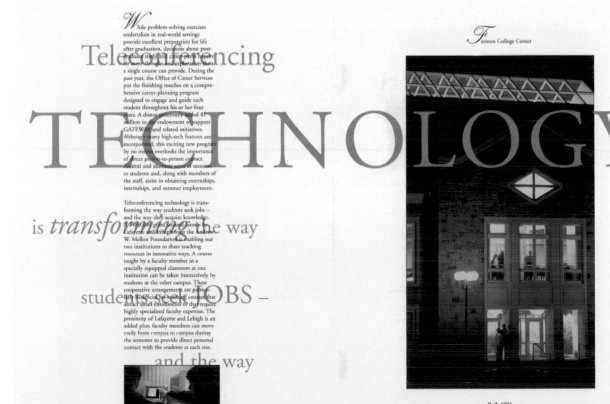

Built 1991

Creative Firm   **Bruce Withers Graphic Design Inc.**
                 New York, New York
Client   *Bruce Withers Graphic Design Inc.*

Perfect binding employs black plastic spiral. Entire brochure is printed on the same weight of white matte paper and trimmed to 8-1/2" x 10-7/8".

The ability to meet objectives and forge
lasting client relationships...

Consistency

◄ Ongoing periodicals... *M* magazine,
published bimonthly for employees and
retirees of Marsh & McLennan Companies...
Fischbach, a quarterly publication
by the Fischbach Corporation, a national
electrical and mechanical contractor.

The ability to translate concepts into strong,
appropriate symbolism...

Vision

► Comprehensive identity programs for
the Coffee, Sugar & Cocoa Exchange,
the Sierra Club and Fischbach Corporation...
identity system for publications of
William M. Mercer's Office of Information
Technology, including the development
of electronic templates and accompanying
applications manual.

mtv networks
more than entertainment
summary of public responsibility

Creative Firm   **MTVN Creative Services**
New York, New York

Client   *MTVN*

Square 6" brochure is printed on white matte stock, cover heavier than text pages. Inside front cover has a vertical pocket with a curved edge.

social/civic/human services

anti-violence

"Nonviolence is the answer to the crucial
political and moral questions of our time."
—Reverend Martin Luther King, Jr.

MTV Networks understands that reducing violence requires reaching out to individuals and motivating them to resolve conflicts peacefully and make their communities SAFe from crime. Our channels—whose audience includes elementary-age children and their parents—have introduced creative, effective programming which addresses violence and hatred in our communities, and offers solutions for coping and prevention. In addition, each channel participates in industry initiatives by airing Public Service Announcements (PSAs) designed to help viewers develop anger management skills and positive behaviors.

05

Voices Against Violence Week: In 1995, MTV Networks participated in this national initiative to raise awareness and offer SoLuTiOns to the problem of rising violence in society. In addition to news segments and special programs, each of our channels aired special signature campaigns for Voices Against Violence as well as

environment

"we should all be concerned about the future
because we will have to spend the rest
of our lives there."
—charles kettering

None of the **AdVANCEs** which cutting-edge
technologies have brought to us will be of any value if we
do not have an Earth on which to live. Since the conception
of MTV Networks, our channels have maintained a
comprehensive environmental awareness campaign to make
our audience more conscious of problems threatening our
environment and the actions we can all take to protect
our planet.

31

Our channels air PSAs which concern clean air/water,
conservation, rainforest **PReSerVaTION**,
endangered species, global warming, pollution,
and recycling.

Earth Day: Every year, our channels produce special
programs, PSAs, and news segments to celebrate Earth Day
and educate the public about the necessities of saving the

arts + culture

"imagination
is more important than knowledge."
—Albert Einstein

MTV Networks has a strong **BONd** with arts and cultural
organizations. Beyond donating air time to organizations
like the National Foundation for the Advancement of the
Arts and the National Cultural Alliance, MTV Networks
purchases paintings and sculptures by young artists to
display in its New York headquarters. The company provides
opportunities for employees to participate in local cultural
events, performances, and shows. The networks also work
with the Rock and Roll Hall of Fame and numerous museums
throughout the country to help reflect rock's cultural and
HISTOriCaL place in society.

37

Creative Firm   **Hornall Anderson Design Works, Inc.**
                   Seattle, Washington
Client   *Novell, Inc.*

Cover of 8-1/2" X 11" brochure is printed on a white glossy stock. Text pages are two different papers. A lighter weight white matte is used alternately with narrow sheets of printed vellum.

Novell has always been at the forefront of [networking] technology. We invented the local-area network, and now we're enabling intranet and Internet computing for thousands of companies. But we know networking isn't just about technology. It's about helping [people] work, learn, and govern more effectively. Our intranet

Novell Solutions

servers provide access to the broadest range of [information.] ManageWise and NDS reduce cost of ownership by making networks easier to manage. GroupWise enables more productive communication and collaboration. Ultimately, these and other products are giving our customers an enduring competitive edge.

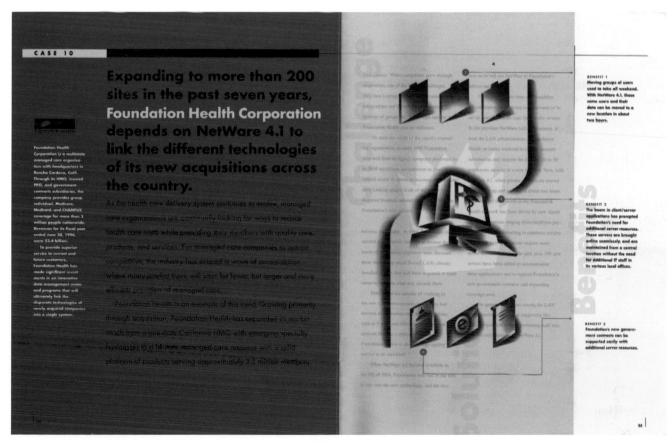

CASE 10

Expanding to more than 200 sites in the past seven years, Foundation Health Corporation depends on NetWare 4.1 to link the different technologies of its new acquisitions across the country.

Creative Firm **Leo Burnett USA**
Chicago, Illinois
Client *United Distillers/*
Johnnie Walker

White gloss stocks are held with a glued binding. Heavier weight than inside paper is used for the cover. Brochure measures 7" square.

"A woman only obliges a man to secrecy, that she may have the pleasure of telling herself."

– William Congreve

Creative Firm   **Dennis S. Juett & Associates Inc.**
             Pasadena, California
Client   *Orion Pictures Corporation*

White semigloss stocks are used in accordance with two vellum pages which are printed with an allover logo pattern. Back inside cover of 8-1/2" x 11" brochure has a pocket flap. Four-color printing with some varnish is utilized.

ORION FEATURE FILMS

Orion Pictures, since its inception, has earned a reputation as a well-known producer and distributor of feature films, encompassing a wide range of genre. Several of its films have surpassed $100 million in box office revenues, including *Amadeus, Platoon, Dances With Wolves* and *The Silence of The Lambs*, each of which has won the Academy Award® for Best Picture. Orion's films have garnered 35 Academy Awards and nearly 100 Academy Award nominations.

Other films of note which are in the Orion film library include: *Dirty Rotten Scoundrels, No Way Out, Colors, Mississippi Burning, Hannah and Her Sisters, Back to School, Cotton Club* and *F/X*.

The Company's motion pictures are distributed to theaters in the United States by its own distribution organization.

Many of Hollywood's most well-known stars have appeared in Orion films. They include Woody Allen, Kevin Costner, Jodie Foster, Gene Hackman, Anthony Hopkins, Paul Newman, Mel Gibson, Sean Penn and Steve Martin.

During the Company's reorganization, which took place in 1992, Orion did not initiate new feature film production; however, the Company did continue to acquire motion pictures from a variety of independent producers for distribution, mainly in North America.

Orion has earned an outstanding reputation among independent producers for its ability to distribute and market feature films in the theatrical, television and home video venues. The Company continues to receive a plethora of submissions from the independent film community, both in script form and completed projects for distribution. In addition, Orion executives attend most major film festivals around the world to seek product which can be acquired for distribution.

The Company's ongoing strategy will focus on both the distribution of independent films and its own production of features, some of which will be co-financed by outside entities. Over the next several years, the Company intends to release an average of 10-12 films per year. Orion will distribute and market these films worldwide, and also derive significant revenues from ancillary markets.

One of the Company's primary objectives in the feature film area will be to increase its market share as a percentage of the industry's total theatrical revenues. Over the years, Orion has continued to enjoy a solid relationship with theater exhibitors who understand that the Orion name creates box office awareness.

Orion's Classics Division acquires, for distribution to theaters, special feature films from a variety of sources, including both foreign and domestic companies. Orion Classics, in recent years, has successfully marketed and distributed films such as *Nostradamus, Boxing Helena* and *Jeffrey*. Orion Classics has a superb reputation for its special niche marketing.

ORION PICTURES INTERNATIONAL

Orion Pictures International (OPI) distributes Orion's product outside of the United States and Canada, in all media. In the foreign pay and free television and home video markets, OPI licenses its product directly to customers in most major territories, and through local sales representatives elsewhere. Theatrical and home video output arrangements with foreign subdistributors have expired, so that OPI is free to control distribution of future product in those media.

OPI will continue to distribute Orion's library in traditional media and established markets, while actively pursuing new areas of exploitation – particularly territories which have not been reached by traditional media and the new markets created by emerging media and technologies, worldwide. OPI also will explore opportunities to acquire and distribute new product in overseas markets, adding freshness and value to the Company's library.

A significant source of revenues for Orion Pictures Corporation is the sales of prerecorded videocassettes to the home video market. The Company's home video operation generates sales by selling Orion's and others' entertainment product to the more than 70,000 video dealers throughout the United States and Canada, as well as to the international marketplace.

The largest percentage of the Company's sales in this venue is done through a number of major home video distributors; in some cases, Orion Home Video sells directly to large retail chain stores in the United States and through sub-distributors in foreign countries.

The growing importance of the home video industry is emphasized by the fact that total consumer spending in the United States in 1994, related to this market, was more than $14 billion, and is expected to be about $19 billion in 1999.

Orion Home Video maintains its own domestic distribution sales force, members of which are located in key market areas throughout the country.

Home video product is obtained directly from Orion Pictures, as well as from several video companies who have exclusive sales agreements with Orion. These companies include Fox Lorber Home Video, well-known for its foreign films, and Major League Baseball Home Video, the leading producer of baseball-related programming. In addition, Orion Home Video has become a leading distributor of a variety of Japanese animation titles. This genre has increased in popularity in recent years.

Orion Home Video provides to the diverse marketplace a variety of product designed to appeal to a wide demographic audience. Millions of videos of Orion's *Dances With Wolves* and *The Silence of The Lambs*, for example, have been purchased by consumers. Unique and creative marketing programs are employed to sustain interest and sales in new video releases, as well as older films from the Orion library.

Orion Home Video, similar to the Company's feature film operation, also acquires titles for distribution from independent companies. Many of these pictures are produced for direct sale to the video market. These are films which do not receive initial play in theaters.

Normally, motion pictures are sold into the home video marketplace six months after theatrical release. The Company has numerous agreements with a variety of independent producers who utilize Orion's sales and marketing expertise to sell their home video product.

In recent years, Orion has negotiated several pacts for the licensing of its feature films to the developing home video new technology arena, including CD-ROM and CD-I; the Company has licensed its films to the home laser disc market for several years.

No matter what new hardware technology is developed in the future – such as the digital video disc – Orion will continue to provide the vital entertainment "software" for the ubiquitous home video market.

Licensing of film and television product from the extensive Orion Pictures Corporation library has provided a stable and predictable stream of revenues for the Company. Orion programming is licensed for television showing to a diverse number of customers in the United States and in most parts of the world.

Customers include the major pay television companies such as Showtime, HBO and Encore; basic cable channels such as the USA Network and Bravo; all of the major television networks; and the television syndication market.

During a period of time prior to 1990, Orion produced and distributed its own original television programming; that activity ceased in 1991, although television programs previously produced by the Company remain available for licensing and generate significant revenues.

Several of the more well-known television series and specials produced by the Company in previous years include: the Emmy® Award winner *Cagney & Lacey*, *Mr. Ed*, *The Kennedys of Massachusetts*, *Green Acres*, *Equal Justice* and *The Murder of Mary Phagan*, for which Jack Lemmon received an Emmy Award.

The Orion name, thanks to the widespread availability of the Company's feature films in the worldwide television market, is well-known and recognized in all parts of the globe, including the emerging markets in Eastern Europe and other countries which previously did not have a significant source of television programming.

Orion Television's future strategy includes the licensing of entertainment product to companies which are developing new technologies such as video on demand. Orion will continue to be an important factor in providing programs for television, whether it be via cable, telephone lines or over the air via satellite.

Licensing of the existing Orion film library, as well as the availability of future feature film product, ensure that the Company will be able to participate in the new communications era, in whatever technology is developed to deliver entertainment to homes throughout the world.

It is projected that by 1999 virtually 100 percent of American households will have at least one television set. As TV penetration similarly increases in other parts of the world, Orion Television will find ready customers for its programming in emerging markets.

Orion Pictures International licenses Company product directly to customers in most major territories for the foreign pay and free television markets. Local sales representatives also are used.

Creative Firm   **Eric Chan Design Co. Ltd.**
                 Hong Kong, China
Client   *Italian Trade Commission*

Spiral-bound brochure's cover has a leather texture to
the stock. The inside pages, measuring 6-3/4" x 10", are
white matte. Some pages are printed four-color process
while other are printed with only one or two match
colors.

Annabella Club
Booth No 132 5th Floor

Via Melitiello, 14   80025 Casandrino (NA)
TEL: (81)5052770   FAX: (81)5054716
CONTACT: Giuseppe Peluso
PRODUCTION: Synthetic ladies' shoes 女裝合成物料鞋
BRANDS: Annabella

Ardena
Booth No 125 5th Floor

Via Circonvallazione Est, 20/a   27023 Cassolnovo (PV)
TEL: (381)929225   FAX: (381)929119
CONTACT: Antonella Covizzoli
SPONSOR: C.C.I.A.A. PAVIA
MEMBERSHIP: VIGEVANO EXPORT
PRODUCTION: High quality/avant garde women's shoes 優質、前衛女裝鞋

Artioli
Booth No 26 5th Floor

Via Oslavia, 3   21049 Tradate (VA)
TEL: (331)841322   FAX: (331)844564
CONTACT: Andrea Artioli
MEMBERSHIP: CONS. CALZ. ITALIANA ALTA MODA
SPONSOR: CONS. CALZ. ITALIANA ALTA MODA
PRODUCTION: Men's shoes, belts and leathergoods 男裝皮鞋、皮帶及皮具系列
BRANDS: Artioli - Antonio Andrea by Artioli
AGENT: Edith Mak-Life Power LTD 7/F Prosperous Commercial Building 54-58 Jardine's Bazaar -
    Causeway Bay HONG KONG - Tel: (852)28080728 Fax: (852)28080872

Astrée
Booth No 33 5th Floor

Via Lecco, 4   20041 Agrate Brianza (MI)
TEL: (331)491734   FAX: (331)551378
CONTACT: Betty Repossini
MEMBERSHIP: CONS. CALZ. ITALIANA ALTA MODA
SPONSOR: CONS. CALZ. ITALIANA ALTA MODA
PRODUCTION: Ladies' shoes 女裝皮鞋
BRANDS: Acteur Mode - Black Heart - Fly Shoes

Attilio
Booth No 72 5th Floor

Via Nicolardi Parco Arcadia, 4/12   80131 Napoli (NA)
TEL: (81)7434000   FAX: (81)7434621
CONTACT: Attilio Palmieri
SPONSOR: CENTRO REG.COMM.EST.CAMPANIA
MEMBERSHIP: CENTRO REG.COMM.EST.CAMPANIA
PRODUCTION: Medium-high quality ladies' shoes 中價優質女裝皮鞋
BRANDS: Attilio

(34)

Linea Zago & Marchiori
Booth No 52 5th Floor

Via Roma 142/A   35020 Saonara (PD)
TEL: (49)640075   FAX: (49)8790415
CONTACT: Francesco Marchiori
SPONSOR: C.E.C.C. DEL VENETO
MEMBERSHIP: Consorzio Maestri Calzaturieri del Brenta
PRODUCTION: Medium/High quality ladies' shoes and bags 中價優質女裝皮鞋及皮袋
BRANDS: La Luna - Zago & Marchiori - Micle - Tre Zeta - Tie In
PROFILE: Ladies' fashion footwear of high quality, with special and particular materials, exclusive
    design. We present also coordinated handbags in colours and materials.

London
Booth No 64 5th Floor

Via Paolo VI   62015 Monte San Giusto (MC)
TEL: (733)837000   FAX: (733)539872
SPONSOR: CENTRO ESTERO C.C.I.A.A. MARCHE
MEMBERSHIP: Consorzio Marche Shoe Group
PRODUCTION: Men's and ladies' sport shoes 男、女裝運動鞋
BRANDS: London

Lorenzo Banfi Milano
Booth No 34 5th Floor

Via Santa Croce, 25   20015 Parabiago (MI)
TEL: (331)553301   FAX: (331)558222
CONTACT: Luca Banfi
PRODUCTION: Footwear and leathergoods 皮鞋及皮具用品
BRANDS: Lorenzo Banfi Milano

Lory
Booth No 98 5th Floor

Via F.Sforza, 63   56028 San Miniato (PI)
TEL: (571)485248   FAX: (571)485166
CONTACT: Luca Martini
PRODUCTION: Medium-high quality ladies' shoes and boots 中價優質女裝皮鞋及皮靴
BRANDS: Franco Martini

Luzzi
Booth No 73 5th Floor

Via Nettuno, 9   52023 Levane - Montevarchi (AR)
TEL: (55)9789905   FAX: (55)9789184
CONTACT: Gennaro Esposito
SPONSOR: Cons.Prod.Calz.Abb.Art.Pelle Aretini
PRODUCTION: Ladies' shoes 女裝皮鞋
BRANDS: Un duex trois

(58)

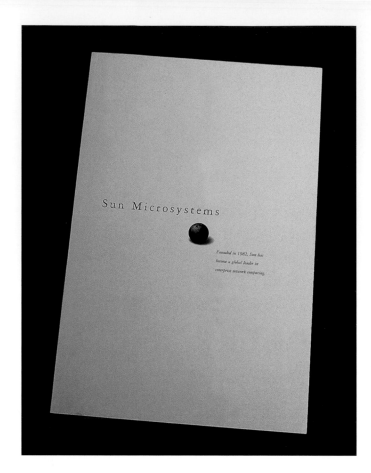

Creative Firm   **Cahan & Associates**
San Francisco, California
Client   *Sun Microsystems*

Utilizing a Velcro closure, an embossed and varnished case houses this brochure. White matte stocks are used throughout, but slightly different color whites. The inside is brighter than the cover. Text pages are 9-3/8" x 14-1/2".

Sprint is a premier provider of telecommunications services to companies ranging from multinational giants to local retail shops. Because we know that the needs of one business are never exactly the same as another, our technological drive has been predicated on developing an advanced network adaptable to companies of every size and complexity.

Using a consultative approach, we invest the time and resources to assess opportunities unique to your business and match them with the right solutions. Flexible, accurate, reliable and secure, the Sprint network is designed to provide customers with virtually every telecommunications service commercially available today — whether you need outbound voice, toll-free service, calling card, electronic messaging and remote access or data solutions such as private lines, frame relay, X.25 packet switching,

ATM or a customized worldwide network for mission-critical applications.

Other innovative products such as *FONVIEW,* a management tool that turns your invoice into a powerful database, and voice *FONCARD,* the calling card that lets your voice do the dialing, reflect our ongoing commitment to enhance your productivity and efficiency.

Your Sprint Representative always works with you to tailor the most effective combination of telecommunication tools for your goals. And as your needs change, Sprint will be there working with you to select the best solutions.

Streamlined Global telecommunications

"Sprint's ultimate objective is to provide real solutions for our customer's business. In partnering with a ski manufacturer, we jointly developed an innovative marketing support program."

Manufacturers today are not only pressured by global competition, but by the need to communicate constantly with employees, field representatives, distributors, sales agents and retailers worldwide.

A manufacturer of specialty sports equipment acquired productivity tools and marketing support through an array of Sprint products. For example, we helped smooth the transition from switched to T1 dedicated outbound access to help cut costs and to add future on-line applications as the business expands. We installed e-mail on their laptops to connect field reps with sales managers and introduced them to Sprint Broadcast Fax enabling simultaneous fax transmission to

Reaching your customers smarter

multiple destinations. The company benefitted from additional time and travel savings by using Sprint's videoconference facility to present its upcoming product line to an overseas subsidiary. Instead of making a 5,000 mile journey, company executives could meet "face to face" with Pacific Rim colleagues and still be home in time for dinner.

Finally, Sprint helped the company jump-start its marketing efforts by suggesting they send pre-paid calling cards imprinted with their own logo to important customers. After a brief "thank-you" from the company, customers use the customized cards to place a free call. At Sprint, value-added service is our specialty.

Sprint continually assesses how people work and learn, access and transfer information, and conduct commerce. We also regularly evaluate technologies to ensure we are providing the best and brightest solutions. In a world where management decisions must rely on a synthesis of ever-changing and complex sources of data, Sprint offers innovative leadership and technological expertise.

That expertise can outfit businesses of all sizes with far-reaching applications. One example is in multimedia, where Sprint is defining the future by exploring broadband interactive applications, ranging from telemedicine and distance learning to simultaneous real-time video editing, home banking and movies-on-demand.

Our joint-ventured PCS licenses are a bold example of bringing new technological solutions to today's demanding business

customers. Unlike the 25-year-old analog technology of cellular, our PCS network will be entirely digital — providing you with the most advanced one-stop shopping for voice and data services.

Our videoconferencing network is the largest in the world. And through telemedia, we are putting automated voice and information response technology to work for you in combination with our toll-free services: applications that can improve customer service, order processing, cost accounting, sales support, advertising and marketing. Most important, they are all engineered to fit your specific needs.

Innovative business leadership

"After spreading its business among several carriers, a high-growth pharmaceutical firm decided that Sprint shared its vision and gave us a long-term contract as its sole service provider."

A fast growing global healthcare company has expanded so rapidly in recent years that its sales offices and production facilities now span 40 countries. In fact, 50 percent of its 5,500 employees and 60 percent of its telecommunications services are now offshore. That meant the company needed more comprehensive, on-line sales and inventory capability, and the ability to manage the escalating costs of more long-distance telephone calls and other data transfer requirements from remote sites into U.S. headquarters.

While Sprint had been the company's voice carrier since 1987, other carriers were handling interna-

Helping your customer faster

tional and data communications. But two years ago, the company decided to consolidate its services and put out an RFP in which one basic criterion was spelled out: to exchange ideas about where the company was heading over the next decade and how telecommunications could best serve its developing needs. In January 1994, the company signed an unprecedented ten-year agreement with Sprint to provide Sprint Virtual Private Network services — connecting all domestic and international locations in a single network — as well as toll-free services. FONCARD, video and messaging world wide. At Sprint, our business is knowing about strategic alliances.

TALENT TREE
Staffing Services

Creative Firm   **Savage Design Group**
                 Houston, Texas
Client   *Talent Tree Staffing Services*

"Master" brochure is really a folder which houses smaller folder-brochures in its back flap pocket. All are printed on white matte paper and use varnish along with ink. Large brochure is 9" x 12". Each smaller brochure is 5" x 10" but unfolds to 15" x 10".

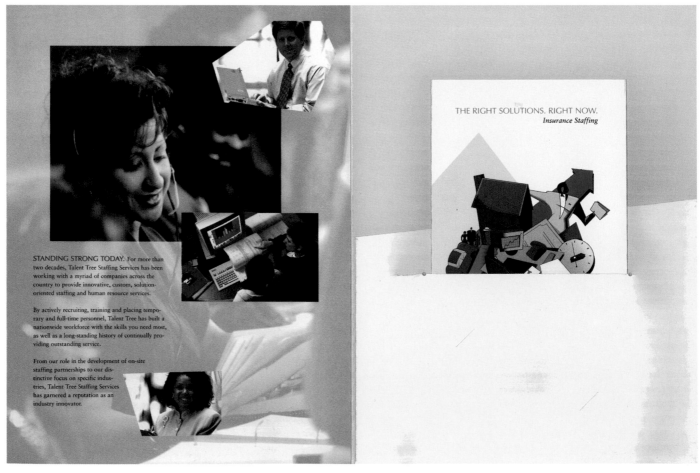

THE RIGHT SOLUTIONS. RIGHT NOW.
Financial Staffing

TALENT TREE
Financial Staffing

THE RIGHT SOLUTIONS. RIGHT NOW.
Healthcare Staffing

TALENT TREE
Healthcare Staffing

THE RIGHT SOLUTIONS. RIGHT NOW.
Telecommunications Staffing

TALENT TREE
Telecom Staffing

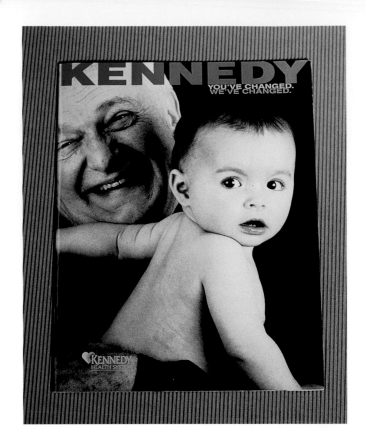

Creative Firm   **Gillespie**
                      Lawrenceville, New Jersey
Client   *Kennedy Health System*

Consistent weight, white matte paper is used for both
brochure's cover and interior. Back inside cover has a
pocket for additional information pieces. Center
spread offers a one-sided foldout. Varnish is used
selectively with other printing in this 8-1/2" x 11"
brochure.

Our dedication to quality care
is matched only by our dedication to advanced technology.

Kennedy has always been committed to providing the very best healthcare in South Jersey. And we've always been dedicated to keeping up with the developments and advancements that change the face of healthcare every day.

How does our commitment translate to better care for you? It means you won't have to travel far from home to get world-class care.

The leading-edge technology at our **Perinatal Testing Units**, for example, provides comprehensive monitoring and testing services for women throughout pregnancy. The units offer some of the most sophisticated fetal diagnostic methods available anywhere, including basic and advanced ultrasound, Doppler blood flow studies, prenatal genetic diagnosis, fetal monitoring, fetal echo-cardiology, and amniocentesis. Kennedy also offers genetic counseling and consultation for patients with high-risk factors like diabetes, hypertension, and Lupus.

Our Muscular Dystrophy Center is the only MDA-sponsored and funded site in South Jersey. It provides diagnostic evaluation and clinical management services for patients with neuromuscular disorders.

Kennedy's Early Intervention Program provides HIV patients with treatment as early as possible to prevent serious illness—and enables them to live healthier lives. The program includes education, counseling, and self-care training, and offers patients the chance to participate in clinical trials of the latest medications and treatments.

Our Dialysis Center provides hemodialysis to patients with end-stage renal disease, and provides training to patients for home dialysis, when appropriate. It is recognized as one of the region's leading dialysis centers by the TransAtlantic Renal Council, an organization appointed by the Federal Health Care Financing Administration, which sets standards for dialysis centers.

As an inpatient or outpatient at Kennedy you'll find
the specialized treatment you need.

There are many ways to access the specialized care you'll receive at Kennedy, and we've dedicated a great deal of our efforts to creating a total health system that addresses your particular medical needs, regardless of the nature or seriousness of the condition.

Our unique **Access Center**, for example, provides a centralized resource for solutions to mental health and/or alcohol and drug abuse problems. Regardless of the severity of the problem, our professionals guide patients into the most appropriate treatment program available, whether it's for detoxification, rehabilitation, or mental health programs for adults, adolescents, and children.

Kennedy's **Family Health Services** makes primary care available to people who are medically under-served, who receive Medicaid or Medicare, or who are under-insured or uninsured. Service centers are located in Somerdale, Chestilhurst, and Washington Township. They provide primary care for children and adults, obstetrics and gynecology, internal medicine, family planning, social services, health education, and substance abuse and nutrition counseling.

Our **Center for Sleep Disorders** provides diagnosis and state-of-the-art treatment to people who have difficulty sleeping, who sleep excessively, who experience fitful drowsiness, or who suffer from sleep apnea.

The Kennedy Teen Center was created to help teenagers make responsible, healthy choices in their lives. To make that goal a reality, the Center provides confidential support, discussion groups, educational material, and medical referrals.

Finally, we offer personalized **Women and Children's Services** for women and their children throughout their lives, including perinatal and maternal care, newborn and pediatric care, and menopause and aging support. For expectant and new mothers, we offer educational programs, breast pump, car seat, and beeper rentals, lactation and nursing training, and baby sitting courses.

For information on our outpatient services, call 1-800-KHS-9097.

Creative Firm   **Mike Salisbury Communications**
                             Torrance, California
Client   *Baja Tours*

Brochure measures 8-1/4" x 11" and is printed on Environment.

The frontier

Whether you're on the popular three-day ride from Ensenada to Mike's Sky Rancho to San Felipe and then back, or if riding the whole peninsula over six days and ending at Cabo San Lucas, Baja Off Road Tours has the route and the itinerary. The only limits are your stamina and desire to ride on this fabulous part of North America. Trips can be customized, and your starting point can be just about any border town you desire.

Riding in Baja California doesn't have to be difficult or worrisome. The extremely scenic riding ranges from coastal plateaus to low desert and everything in-between. Folklore has it that the deserts of Baja can be treacherous, and while some of that folklore is probably true, Baja Off Road Tours takes out the treachery and the worry. Here you can concentrate on your riding, enjoy your foray onto undisturbed wilderness and celebrate your hard-ridden miles. With Chris' fifteen years of experience comes a calm and instinct for getting even the absolute novice through some very wonderful, yet possibly challenging country.

You'll find a charm in the many villages and towns you'll see and you'll experience the warmth of the Mexican people. If you're a connoisseur of Mexican food, then you might just find yourself in culinary Heaven. With traditional continental cuisine offered at three- and four star restaurants in Ensenada, wonderful home-cooked barbecues at Mike's Sky Rancho, and platters of prawns and other delectable seafood in San Felipe, about all else you'll need is a frothy Mexican beer or an ice-cold margarita. All accommodations are U.S. Standard and feature full bathrooms and bottled water in each room.

Riding in Baja is not punishing or difficult. Anyone with enough savvy to shift gears and keep their balance can handle the trails and roads here. Chris tailors Baja Off Road trips to the experience level of the group. You're assured that you won't get in over your head or go away wanting more. Chris runs three trips per month on average. The most requested is the three-day upper peninsula ride. It includes almost all the things and features the best riding areas in Baja. On this trip you'll ride the mountains, the coast, the desert, a dry lake and even in a pine forest. Of course, riding wouldn't nearly be as much fun here if you didn't get an occasional water crossing...

You'll never have to worry about feeling left out in a large group because one-on-one attention and small group riding are what this Off Road Tours are all about. Optimum sized groups help keep riding times intact, help keep the dust down and also help everyone to get to know one another more quickly.

Baja Off Road Tours runs fully guided and escorted routes. You'll never have to rely on a map, a compass or ever get lost. Chris escorts almost all trips and has one of his staff maintain the "sweep" position at the end of the group. In addition to these obvious safety precautions, Baja Off Road Tours has all of its trips followed by chase vehicles. Whether they're for bringing lunch or beverages to the most outrageous lunch stops, or acting as a portable tool box and machine shop, the chase vehicles also offer you, the rider, a refuge should you need a break for a few hours.

An honorary citizen of Ensenada, Baja California, Mexico. A legendary, award-winning factory mechanic. A fierce competitor and Baja class winner. An expert on riding in Baja and in giving first-timers a first-class experience.

Chris Haines, also known in the Baja Peninsula as "Señor Chris," brings not only an understanding of the expanses, terrain and challenges of Baja to his operation, but also a camaraderie with its people. Chris is no stranger to Baja; he's competed here, wrenched here and won here. He knows where the best trails are, how to get his party safely through them and how to match off road riders with riding areas that aptly suit their abilities. In short, he and his team will do all the work for you so that you can concentrate on riding and having a good time.

Chris is no stranger to keeping things running either. With over 15 years experience as a top-level factory tuner, Chris has worked with such notable National and World Champions as Bruce Penhall, Tony DiStefano, Brian Myerscough, Darrel Schultz, Ron Lechien, Danny Laporte and Mickey Dymond. Along with helping these Speedway, Motocross and Off-Road superstars, Chris earned his own accolades along the way as a four time A.M.A. Golden Wrench winner and six time Motocross des Nations factory motocross tuner.

It shouldn't be surprising that Baja Off Road Tours has been featured twice on "Motoworld" and that they hold an annual celebrity ride each Spring. In his own right Chris can compete with the best too. He's garnered class wins in the Baja 1000 and Baja 500, along the way accumulating five Baja 1000 race wins totaling thirteen finishes and two S.C.O.R.E. class championships. His experience in Baja benefits all of his riders. He can offer advice and tips on technique, practice and running the desert at racing speeds.

A resident of California with bases in Southern California and Ensenada, Mexico, Chris splits his time between the two countries. Since the cooler months are the best for riding in Baja, it's not surprising that October through May are Chris' busiest months.

chris haines

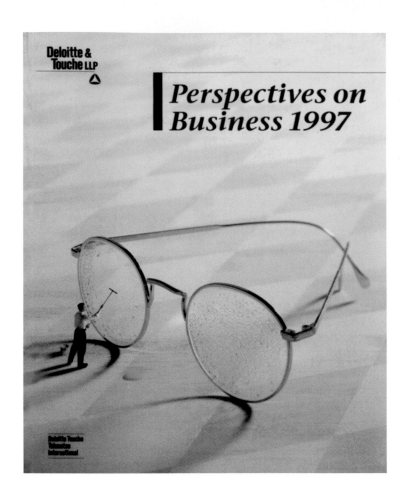

Creative Firm   **Addison**
                 New York, New York
Client   *Deloitte & Touche*

Four-color process in accordance with some metallic ink were used on white matte stocks in this 9" x 11" brochure.

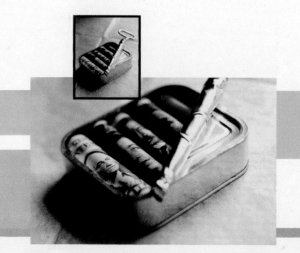

Ready, Set, Grow

by Thomas L. Doorley III and Gerald B. Mendelbaum

fig. a

In the wake of a torrent of downsizings and the relentless emphasis on cost containment, a new priority is emerging in the boardrooms of today's leading companies: growth. According to a recent Deloitte & Touche survey of *Fortune* 1000 executives, 85 percent of the respondents ranked growth a strategic priority for their company. That's not surprising, considering that growth companies achieve sharply higher performance in the areas that matter most—to their investors, their employees, their customers, and the economy:

For **investors**, the top 20 percent of growing companies create $5 of value for each $1 the bottom 20 percent generate.

For **employees**, job satisfaction at growth companies runs high, despite longer hours and more pressure to deliver results.

For **customers**, growth companies develop innovative and cheaper products.

For **the economy**, growth companies comprise the job-creating engine. A mere 100 growth companies have created one in five of the U.S. jobs this decade.

Tax Reform: The Measures of Success

by Roger L. Page and C. Chandk Sittich

Creative Firm   **Chermayeff & Geismar, Inc.**
                          Bennington, New Hampshire
Client   *Monadnock Paper Mills, Inc.*

Brochure measures 9" x 12" and is printed on Monadnock
Astrolite (bright white) cover 65 lb. Besides CMYK, inks include
three PMS colors and a gloss varnish.

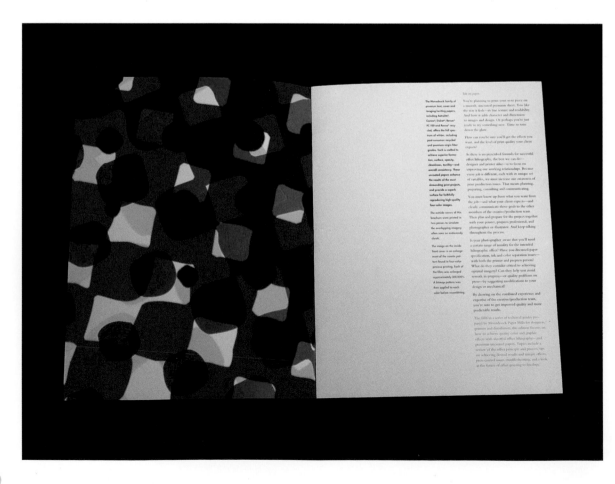

Creative Firm   **Peterson & Company**
                              Dallas, Texas
Client   *The Dallas Society of Visual Communications*

Large brochure (11" x 15") is bound across the top with heavy duty staples and a corrugated cardboard strip. Front cover is printed on brown cardboard. Using black and one other color ink, inside pages and back cover are white matte stock.

"Tom had asked his dentist's receptionist to stop by to have some test shots done. When I answered the door, this very pretty brunette was standing there and said, 'My name is Jane Russell.'"

It was also while he was at R&S that Marvin met his future wife, Joy. "The editor invited her to come along to lunch, and that's how we met—and it's been the Fourth of July ever since."

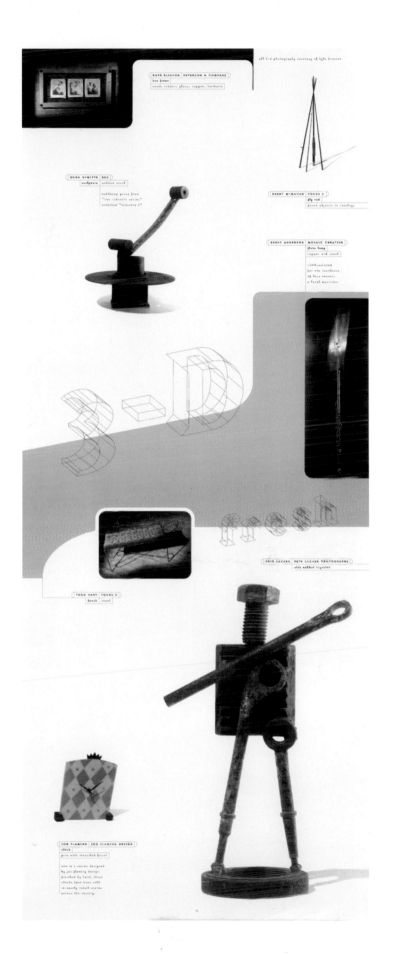

Antista Fairclough Design

Creative Firm **Antista Fairclough Design**
Atlanta, Georgia
Client *Antista Fairclough Design*

Large 11-1/2" x 15" brochure employs staggered pages for interesting visual effect. A variety of fibered stocks and white glossy paper were used with four-color process, match colors, and varnish.

The Store

Four thousand square feet of merchandise and 3-dimensional visual graphics help create a unique environment for customers. Although the store looks expensive, it was designed with close consideration of cost parameters. All graphic elements were designed and value engineered from the start.

Interior

LARGE FOOD AND BEVERAGE ICONS CIRCLE THE VAULTED CEILING

FRESH DAIRY & JUICES

The interior development was based on creating a true retail environment for the customer. The fresh-produce cart reinforces a more inviting atmosphere. The wall signage makes it easy for the customer to readily locate the different product areas of the store.

126

Branding

Retail, branding and packaging become stronger when developed together under an umbrella called identity. SnG used this concept to develop an overall visual consistency to convey its "identity" to the consumer.

&Packaging

ICE BAGS, MATCHBOOKS AND CUPS ARE AMUNG MANY OF THE BRANDED PACKAGES

Impact

Branding is a powerful tool that conveys who you are to the consumer. SnG's branded packaging displays its new logo with a new graphic image that consists of product icons and a color palette that is used throughout the store's interior and exterior applications.

Speed

CONVENIENCE FOR THE CUSTOMER IS KEY. PAYING AT THE PUMP ALLOWS THE CUSTOMER TO GET IN AND OUT QUICKLY. THIS MEANS THAT ADVERTISING AND VENDING AT THE PUMP BECOMES A KEY ISSUE.

Sign of the times

GO POWER
GP
2000

The GP is GP 2000 stands for Go Power and Guaranteed Performance. Go Power represents because fuel timeliness is an important factor to the customer.

Creative Firm   **Savage Design Group**
                 Houston, Texas
Client   *Champagne Printing*

Spiral-bound brochure is printed on a total of six different types of paper. Cover uses perfect binding along with debossing and silver foil stamping. Gloss varnish is printed over photographs throughout. Overall size is 8-1/2" x 12".

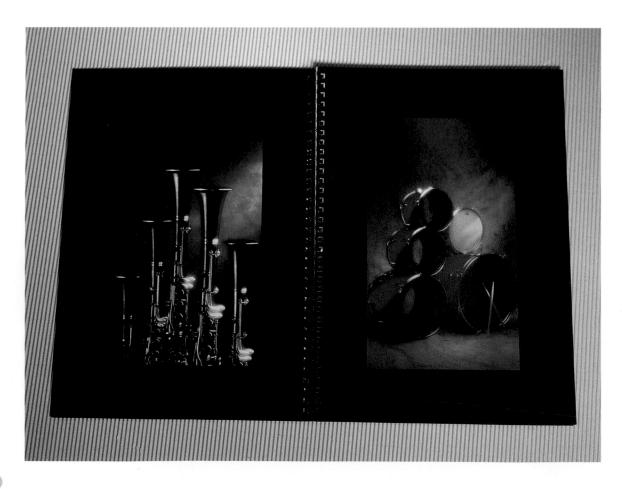

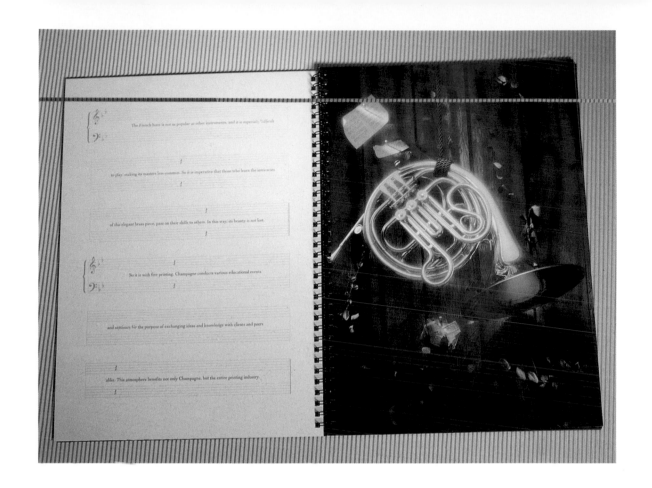

129

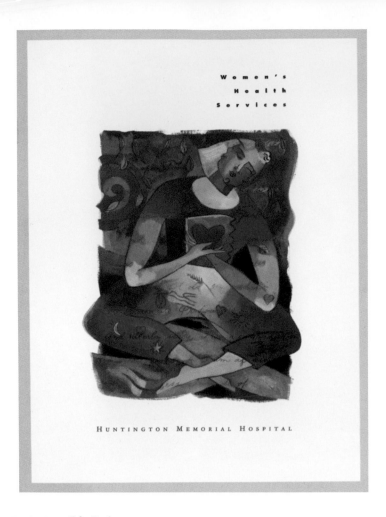

Women's Health Services

HUNTINGTON MEMORIAL HOSPITAL

Creative Firm   **Erbe Design**
             S. Pasadena, California
Client   *Huntington Memorial Hospital*

This brochure is 7-3/4" x 10-1/4". Cover and text pages are printed on the same weight of white dull paper. Inside back cover offers a pocket (with business card cuts) with a curved corner.

"There was so much I wanted to know when I first got pregnant. So I took some of their classes and felt like an expert even before the baby was born."

State-of-the-art medicine from members of your community.

Huntington Hospital is the acknowledged leader in medical technology, services, and facilities in the San Gabriel Valley. But we're also active members of a vital, diverse community, whose health and well-being is more than just a matter of professional concern. It is the health and well-being of neighbors, friends, families—newcomers and long-time residents alike.

We provide the community with advanced, appropriate, compassionate care, in our own facilities and through our relationships with the top medical professionals in the area. But we also strive to prevent illness, to in fact, promote wellness, through education, information and involvement in the development and maintenance of healthy lifestyles. In addition, we have taken on the role of advocate for women's health issues, encompassing every stage of a woman's life.

Women's health: It's more than just having babies.

At Huntington Hospital, we give equal weight to each stage of life and its accompanying health concerns—from the childbearing years, through midlife, through the senior years. We're committed to helping you meet the different challenges, problems and opportunities you face, with optimal health, no matter how old, or young, you are.

The childbearing years.

Whether you have children or not, your body is designed for that function. And during the childbearing years, your reproductive organs will, of course, play a role in your overall health.

The Huntington Reproductive Center.

It could be an important resource for you. The Huntington Reproductive Center is a collaboration between Huntington Hospital and a renowned group of reproductive endocrinologists, infertility specialists, and clinical and laboratory experts in reproductive medicine. Together they have, in a relatively short time, built an international reputation for their ability to correct infertility. In fact, their success rate is near double the national average.

In a state-of-the-art facility, the group employs a unique family approach to correcting infertility, often treating both partners simultaneously. A wide variety of treatment options is available, but individual programs are tailored to the specific needs of the couple, from counseling to conception.

Healthy mother. Healthy child.

Before you even become pregnant, we at Huntington Hospital are thinking of ways to help you prepare for what will be one of the most important events of your life.

We have a program called Parent Path® for couples who are thinking about starting a family. It includes informational/educational events, and newsletters filled with advice on financial planning, nutrition, creating a nursery in your home, and more. We conduct tours of the hospital's obstetrical areas and arrange meetings with obstetricians who can answer your questions. So that when you do become pregnant, you'll be ready.

I grow older, not old.

I am ambitious. And humble.

Profoundly serious. And utterly silly.

I am a contradiction. And an open book.

I am afraid. I am fearless. I am all of these.

You are a woman. And whether you came of age in this, the last decade of the twentieth century, or fifty years ago, you're unlike any woman who came before you. You're more independent, better educated, and probably healthier than your mother and grandmothers. You deal with issues they never dreamed of. You care for children and parents, often simultaneously. When faced with health concerns, you're an active partner in the search for solutions. And you expect your health services to combine cutting edge medical science with compassion and respect. In the San Gabriel Valley, that means Huntington Memorial Hospital.

131

disease and stroke in women are of primary concern to us. Our cardiology services, for women as well as men, include prevention, advanced diagnosis, medical and surgical intervention

earned an international reputation. It reaches out to seniors with a newsletter and educational programs on nutrition, weight management, and smoking cessation, as well as others that encourage

"Jack was so sick for so long, I was completely worn out when he died. But I'm still here... they tell me I'm healthy as a horse, so now I'm making a new life for myself."

"I've always believed you're never too old to try something new. So I'm learning to swim. At 73!"

Huntington Hospital's obstetrical and neonatal services are unmatched in the San Gabriel Valley. When you choose Huntington as the place to have your baby, we first refer you to a qualified obstetrician, if you don't already have one. We offer classes in Lamaze childbirth techniques, breastfeeding, nutrition, cesarean delivery, infant and child CPR and exercise. We'll invite you to become a member of Our First® or Our New Addition® programs, which provide information, a newsletter and a membership card that entitles you to discounts from local merchants on clothes and other purchases for yourself and your baby.

We maintain the highest levels of experience and technology in perinatology (high-risk pregnancies) and neonatology (the care of premature or severely ill newborns). Our obstetrical

department contains combined labor, delivery and recovery rooms (LDRs), eliminating the need to be moved from room to room during birth. After delivery, we provide Couplet Care, in which you and your baby share the same nursing team during your hospital stay, so you have more quality time together.

Smart parenting.

Being a parent is a big job, one for which almost nobody feels very qualified at the start. We can help. We offer educational, immunization and outreach programs for young families. Our staff includes a wide range of pediatric specialists as well as certified child life specialists to help you and your children cope with the emotional aspects of a serious illness, the birth of a sibling, death of a parent, or anything else that

involves children and hospitals. Huntington's emergency room is designated by the County of Los Angeles for both general and critical pediatric care and the staff is trained to respond to the unique needs of sick and frightened children. Our pediatric intensive care unit (PICU) is staffed with physicians who are specialists in pediatric intensive care.

We're also making those minor, inevitable childhood injuries and illnesses easier to handle with Huntington HealthExpress. It's an urgent care center staffed with welltrained, experienced pediatric and family health nurse practitioners. We think you'll find the services of Huntington HealthExpress compassionate, efficient and affordable.

And if you like, we can refer you to a qualified pediatrician, as well.

Midlife: A time of change. For the better.

It's a time of changing bodies, changing lifestyles, changing priorities. It can be the most productive, most satisfying time of your life, a time of self-discovery, self-knowledge, perhaps a bit of long-deferred self-indulgence. What midlife most certainly is not is that mythical age of decline. You have a lot of choices to make, a lot of living to do. Which is why we at Huntington Hospital want to help you become an educated health care consumer.

We are, for instance, acutely aware of the confusion caused by the controversy about hormone replacement therapy (HRT). So we want to help you talk intelligently with your gynecologist about

loved ones, as you age.

Senior Care Network.

It's Huntington Hospital's community program for seniors. Its centerpiece is the training, support and relief of caregivers, for which the program has

nation's health. Huntington Hospital has long understood this, and has given the issue the attention it warrants. If you'd like to know more about Women's Health Services at Huntington Memorial Hospital, please call us at 1-800-820-3463.

The facts about women's health.

Enclosed is important information.

Take a first step in maintaining a healthy lifestyle

by becoming an educated health care consumer.

We've included a list of health topics that may interest you

and we'll be happy to send you this information.

So call us at 1-800-820-3463.

133

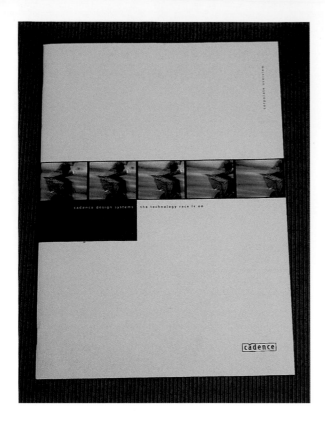

Creative Firm   **Oh Boy, A Design Company**
                       San Francisco, California
Client   *Cadence Design Systems*

Brochure is 8-1/4" x 11-5/8", and is printed on white matte
cover stock throughout. Back inside cover offers a foldout.
Several pages have perforations which invite the viewer to tear
and create different characters with a melange of photos.

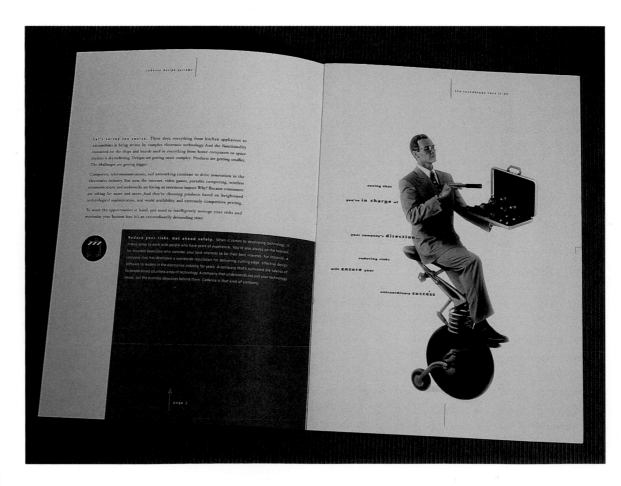

In less than five years
over 25% of the American workforce
will become telecommuters.

Creative Firm   **Peterson & Company**
                 Dallas, Texas
Client   *Data Race*

Cover and inside pages are printed on the same weight of white matte
stock. Inside back cover has a pocket with a stepped-cut edge. Overall size
is 9" x 12".

And nobody
is better positioned than we are
to make this emerging market more productive.

Data Race can put a world of
information at your
fingertips.

DATA RACE

136

At DATA RACE, our business is to provide your company with the tools to succeed in today's information driven economy. We are an innovator and world leader in providing remote access to the corporate environment. DATA RACE has already achieved a solid reputation with our ability to create innovative and unique communications solutions that challenge all existing ground rules. We are re-defining business communications with products that include the world's only line of custom OEM modems offering integrated voice capabilities, a full duplex speaker phone, telephone answering machine, fax answering and much more. Additionally, we offer a revolutionary new approach to remote branch office multi-plexing, with a product line based on a unique multiprocessor design that ensures your investment won't become obsolete as new technologies such as ISDN, ATM, T1/E1 and Frame Relay become available.

Building a foundation for an information driven economy: why DATA RACE has the edge.

None of the products we make is an end in itself. They are modular building blocks that can be used to build a total communications solution. Our mission is to provide complete, integrated access to the corporate information environment. By offering the world's most advanced notebook computer modems and a flexible new open systems approach to remote office multiplexing, DATA RACE has established a firm foundation for continuing our leadership role in providing the information solutions that business needs to succeed in an information-based economy.

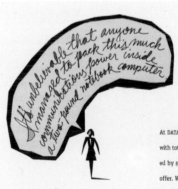

At DATA RACE, our philosophy of providing business with total communication solutions is best illustrated by some of the innovative products we already offer. We are the only manufacturer in the world offering a 28.8Kbps OEM notebook computer modem featuring full duplex voice capabilities, an integrated full duplex speaker phone, digital telephone answering machine, automated fax answering and much more. Over 100,000 people are already using advanced DATA RACE modems to access their entire corporate information environment. With a complete communication center inside their notebook computer that allows them to send and receive voice calls, check their voice and e-mail, send and receive faxes and access their data network at any time, these users are crucial minutes, hours, and even days ahead of their competition.

Multiplexing is a powerful communications tool that can offer significant savings for any business with remote locations, often eliminating the need for separate, and very expensive, dedicated lines for voice, fax, and data. Combining voice, fax, and data to branch offices over one line allows the end user to relay more traffic over fewer lines, resulting in greater capability at substantially lower costs.

The thing that sets DATA RACE multiplexing solutions apart from competitors is a unique modular multiprocessor design that makes it easy to upgrade capacity whenever necessary to meet increased system demands. DATA RACE network multiplexers can connect as few as two up to several hundred branch offices, to your home office, by sharing voice, fax, data, and LAN bridging over the same lines. And, when migrating from 56Kbps to ISDN, ATM, Frame Relay or T1/E1 service, the DATA RACE modular design ensures easy upgradability which protects your initial investment.

Innovative products that are changing the way business communicates.

137

We are on a journey...

PHAMIS
INCORPORATED

Creative Firm   **Phinney/Bischoff Design House**
                 Seattle, Washington
Client   *PHAMIS, Inc.*

Monochromatic photographs printed on white matte stock are the signature of this 8-3/4" x 11-3/4" brochure. Back inside cover has flap to hold additional information.

shared vision

Today, integrated delivery systems across the nation have chosen to work with PHAMIS Inc. for two key reasons: We have more than 20 years of experience developing enterprise-wide information solutions and a long-standing reputation for cultivating strong partnerships with our clients.

Our ultimate goal? To help you harness the power of information in order to gain insights into your patient population and organization—insights that can ultimately lead to improved outcomes, greater patient satisfaction and decreased costs.

As providers of comprehensive information systems for patient care and enterprise management, we offer our clients, among which are some of the nation's most respected healthcare

organizations, the tools they need to access strategic and clinical information: Information they need at every step to realize their vision.

But more importantly, we're in the business of supporting you in your goal of improving the delivery of healthcare. Toward this end, we will help you overcome obstacles in your path to surviving—and succeeding—in today's cost-driven healthcare marketplace.

"PHAMIS Inc. gives us the ability to pursue our vision."

"Anticipating a minimum 10-year relationship with our information systems provider, we placed a great deal of emphasis on how the vendor's vision matched ours. Because PHAMIS Inc. is moving in the same direction with us, we are confident that they will offer all of the capabilities we need to carry out our strategic vision."

The key to building successful relationships is collaboration—the foundation of our Signature Service. From business planning through system implementation, a team of product, technical and clinical experts is assigned to your project. At every stage, we work closely with your team to combine strengths and achieve optimal results. In addition, one of our senior executives works directly with your senior management, providing ongoing consultation and problem-solving.

Through extensive discussions with clients early on, we seek to understand the organization's challenges, strategies and priorities in order to deliver solutions based upon solving real business problems. By identifying what takes precedence, we can structure system implementation to maximize benefits at each phase. For example, phase one can provide population characteristics, disease registries and health screening data to help you better manage your patient base. Subsequent phases can continue to enhance and build on those capabilities.

Sponsoring regular events that give clients the opportunity to network, share best practices and exchange ideas with each other and with our team is an equally important part of our Signature Service. These events include executive forums, physician advisory groups, focus groups, special conferences and the PHAMIS Inc. Users Network. On a regular basis, we also conduct telephone surveys to measure client satisfaction and, as necessary, initiate service improvements based upon client feedback.

This approach to service and to client relationships fosters a collaborative environment in which all team members are able to join together, unified in their quest for excellence by a sense of shared purpose and vision.

"At any time, I can call Frank Sample, the CEO at PHAMIS Inc. We have an open, honest relationship—a real partnership for the future."

"I feel a very strong chemistry between our team and PHAMIS Inc., all the way from the CEO to the technicians involved on a daily basis."

In the late 1970s, our founders, Drs. Malcolm Gieser and Mark Wheeler, envisioned a longitudinal electronic medical record that could track patient care across the care continuum over multiple delivery sites. Early LASTWORD® clients have collected years of valuable patient information and are using it to their strategic advantage.

Today, our clients recognize that their ability to reduce costs and improve outcomes depends upon having access to robust patient information. As they move forward, they also understand the importance of working in partnership with us to get the most from their information system tools—tools that will help them achieve their objectives.

Our ongoing collaboration with clients has led us to expand our offering from one to three product lines. These include:

LASTWORD®: Our solution for integrated healthcare delivery captures patient-centered information, building an electronic medical record as an outcome of workflow automation and supporting enterprise-wide decisions about population care, process improvements and demand management.

DATABREEZE™: Our solution for provider management, DATABREEZE, delivers the information required to successfully manage patient care, operations and managed care programs for large physician groups.

ENTERPRISE VIEW™: Our outcomes repository system delivers enterprise-wide information for strategic analysis, helping clients improve health status, increase patient satisfaction, optimize utilization and manage competitive market positioning.

As our clients seek more effective ways to reduce costs and improve outcomes, we will continue to view their ideas as a critical part of developing solutions that support their business objectives. This approach gives our clients a sense of ownership in the solution and sets the stage for mutual success.

"PHAMIS Inc. sees the future of healthcare the same way we see it."

"The leadership at PHAMIS Inc. thinks at the same strategic level as we do. So solutions are focused on meeting our business needs, not just today—but 10 years down the road."

Creative Firm   **Lindsay Smithers - FCB Impact**
Johannesburg, South Africa
Client   *Ster Kinekor*

Printed on white matte papers and vellum, this large (11-5/8" x 16-1/2") brochure comes in a card case. Silver metallic ink is used on the cover.

It seems natural to give over to your body's involuntary impulses when cheap cider or food poisoning are responsible. but when the only reason you can think of is the few flickering fantasy images in front of you, it is terrifying.

THEN

Jayne Mansfield

Entering our lives at different intervals, we live by them, for them, and with them. Offering escapism, true life drama, comedy, tragedy, horror and delight, in reality or fantasy our lives would not be the same without **them**

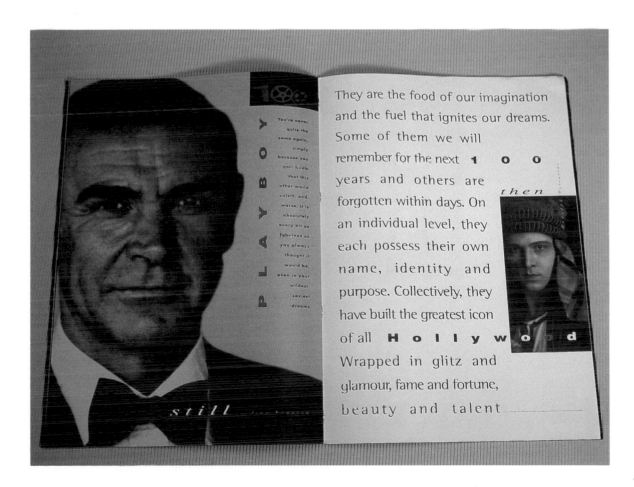

PLAYBOY

You're never quite the same again, simply because you now know that this other world exists, and, worse, it is absolutely every bit as fabulous as you always thought it would be, even in your wildest, sexiest dreams

still

They are the food of our imagination and the fuel that ignites our dreams. Some of them we will remember for the next **1 0 0** years and others are forgotten within days. On an individual level, they each possess their own name, identity and purpose. Collectively, they have built the greatest icon of all **Hollywood** Wrapped in glitz and glamour, fame and fortune, beauty and talent_____

then

Creative Firm   **Principal Communications**
                     New York, New York
Client   *GE Capital*

Four-color process printing, metallic ink, and varnish are
utilized on white glossy stock in this 8" x 13".

*"We have created a seamless organi-
zation with a global perspective,
able to focus unparalleled resources
to serve the changing needs of a
recovering airline industry."*

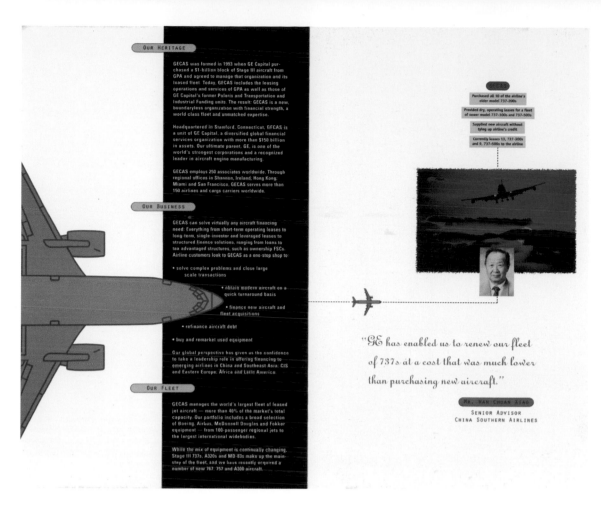

Our Heritage

GECAS was formed in 1993 when GE Capital purchased a $1-billion block of Stage III aircraft from GPA and agreed to manage that organization and its leased fleet. Today, GECAS includes the leasing operations and services of GPA as well as those of GE Capital's former Polaris and Transportation and Industrial Funding units. The result: GECAS is a new, boundaryless organization with financial strength, a world class fleet and unmatched expertise.

Headquartered in Stamford, Connecticut, GECAS is a unit of GE Capital, a diversified global financial services organization with more than $150 billion in assets. Our ultimate parent, GE, is one of the world's strongest corporations and a recognized leader in aircraft engine manufacturing.

GECAS employs 250 associates worldwide. Through regional offices in Shannon, Ireland, Hong Kong, Miami and San Francisco, GECAS serves more than 150 airlines and cargo carriers worldwide.

Our Business

GECAS can solve virtually any aircraft financing need. Everything from short-term operating leases to long-term, single-investor and leveraged leases to structured finance solutions, ranging from loans to tax advantaged structures, such as ownership FSCs. Airline customers look to GECAS as a one-stop shop to:

- solve complex problems and close large scale transactions
- obtain modern aircraft on a quick turnaround basis
- finance new aircraft and fleet acquisitions
- refinance aircraft debt
- buy and remarket used equipment

Our global perspective has given us the confidence to take a leadership role in offering financing to emerging airlines in China and Southeast Asia; CIS and Eastern Europe, Africa and Latin America.

Our Fleet

GECAS manages the world's largest fleet of leased jet aircraft — more than 40% of the market's total capacity. Our portfolio includes a broad selection of Boeing, Airbus, McDonnell Douglas and Fokker equipment — from 100-passenger regional jets to the largest international widebodies.

While the mix of equipment is continually changing, Stage III 737s, A320s and MD-83s make up the mainstay of the fleet, and we have recently acquired a number of new 767, 757 and A300 aircraft.

GECAS

Purchased all 10 of the airline's older model 737-200s

Provided dry, operating leases for a fleet of newer model 737-300s and 737-500s

Supplied new aircraft without tying up airline's credit

Currently leases 13, 737-300s and 9, 737-500s to the airline

"GE has enabled us to renew our fleet of 737s at a cost that was much lower than purchasing new aircraft."

MR. HAN CHUAN XIAO
SENIOR ADVISOR
CHINA SOUTHERN AIRLINES

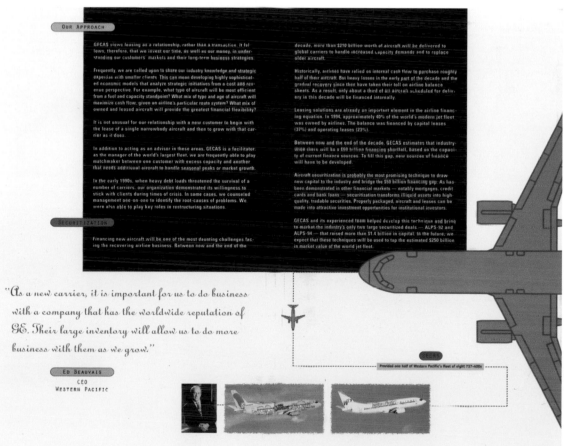

Our Approach

GECAS views leasing as a relationship, rather than a transaction. It follows, therefore, that we invest our time, as well as our money, in understanding our customers' markets and their long-term business strategies.

Frequently, we are called upon to share our industry knowledge and strategic expertise with smaller clients. This can mean developing highly sophisticated economic models that analyze strategic initiatives from a cost and revenue perspective. For example, what type of aircraft will be most efficient from a fuel and capacity standpoint? What mix of type and age of aircraft will maximize cash flow, given an airline's particular route system? What mix of owned and leased aircraft will provide the greatest financial flexibility?

It is not unusual for our relationship with a new customer to begin with the lease of a single narrowbody aircraft and then to grow with that carrier as it does.

In addition to acting as an advisor in these areas, GECAS is a facilitator: as the manager of the world's largest fleet, we are frequently able to play matchmaker between one customer with excess capacity and another that needs additional aircraft to handle seasonal peaks or market growth.

In the early 1990s, when heavy debt loads threatened the survival of a number of carriers, our organization demonstrated its willingness to stick with clients during times of crisis. In some cases, we counseled management one-on-one to identify the root-causes of problems. We were also able to play key roles in restructuring situations.

Securitization

Financing new aircraft will be one of the most daunting challenges facing the recovering airline business. Between now and the end of the decade, more than $210 billion worth of aircraft will be delivered to global carriers to handle increased capacity demands and to replace older aircraft.

Historically, airlines have relied on internal cash flow to purchase roughly half of their aircraft. But heavy losses in the early part of the decade and the gradual recovery since then have taken their toll on airline balance sheets. As a result, only about a third of all aircraft scheduled for delivery in this decade will be financed internally.

Leasing solutions are already an important element in the airline financing equation. In 1994, approximately 40% of the world's modern jet fleet was owned by airlines. The balance was financed by capital leases (37%) and operating leases (23%).

Between now and the end of the decade, GECAS estimates that industry-wide there will be a $50 billion financing shortfall, based on the capacity of current finance sources. To fill this gap, new sources of finance will have to be developed.

Aircraft securitization is probably the most promising technique to draw new capital to the industry and bridge the $50 billion financing gap. As has been demonstrated in other financial markets — notably mortgages, credit cards and bank loans — securitization transforms illiquid assets into high-quality, tradable securities. Properly packaged, aircraft and leases can be made into attractive investment opportunities for institutional investors.

GECAS and its experienced team helped develop this technique and bring to market the industry's only two large securitized deals — ALPS-92 and ALPS-94 — that raised more than $1.4 billion in capital. In the future, we expect that these techniques will be used to tap the estimated $250 billion in market value of the world jet fleet.

"As a new carrier, it is important for us to do business with a company that has the worldwide reputation of GE. Their large inventory will allow us to do more business with them as we grow."

ED BEAUVAIS
CEO
WESTERN PACIFIC

GECAS

Provided one half of Western Pacific's fleet of eight 737-300s

Creative Firm   **OXO International**
                 New York, New York
Client   *OXO International*

Various recycled papers are successfully employed in the printing of this brochure measuring 9" x 11-1/2". Cover and full text pages are smooth white stock. "Half" text pages are tan, dull paper. White paper is printed with four-color process, while tan is printed with black and one match color. Inside back cover offers half-page, flap pocket.

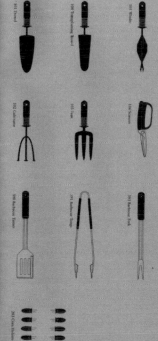

Safety and sleekness blend together beautifully in our GOOD GRIPS Tea Kettle. Carefully crafted to keep steam and heat away from your hands, our kettle makes pouring a cup of tea as relaxing as sipping it.

When we set out to introduce our version of this kitchen classic, we wanted it to be as safe and practical as possible. So we built in an innovative steam shield. The handle is positioned to a lower center of gravity for reduced wrist strain when pouring. The wide lid snaps on and makes for easy cleaning and the spout cap locks open for easy filling and pouring. And yes, it whistles, too. Available in stainless steel, or black, white, green or blue enamel, it's unique, it's attractive, and it is the most practical kettle around.

We take time to research and test our tools — from our first Peeler to our latest addition — so that we can bring our customers the highest quality products. They know that OXO means quality, comfort and value.

| 71081 | 71082 | 71084 | 71083 |
| Jet Black | Polar White | Hunter Green | Cobalt Blue |

71080
Stainless Steel (opposite)

101 Trowel / 104 Transplanting Trowel / 105 Weeder
102 Cultivator / 103 Fork / 106 Shears
106 Barbecue Turner / 201 Barbecue Tongs / 201 Barbecue Fork
265 Corn Holders

Creative Firm   **Ce Diseña**
                Santiago, Chile
Client   *Tironi & Asociados*

Brochure made very much like a book
measures 10-5/8" x 10-1/2". Spiral
binding is encased in a hard cover. Lots
of 3/4 sheets of printed vellum and 1/4
sheets of printed white semigloss stock
are interspersed among the pages.

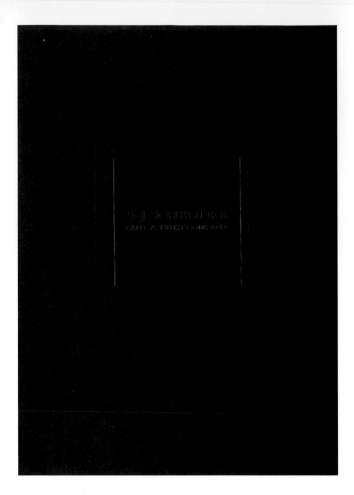

Creative Firm **Taylor & Ives Incorporated**
New York, New York
Client *IBJ Schroder Bank & Trust Company*

Brochure cover is textured, fibered, ecru stock. It is printed, blind embossed, and gold foiled stamped. First and last pages of 8-1/4" x 11-3/4" brochure are printed vellum. Text pages are white glossy stock.

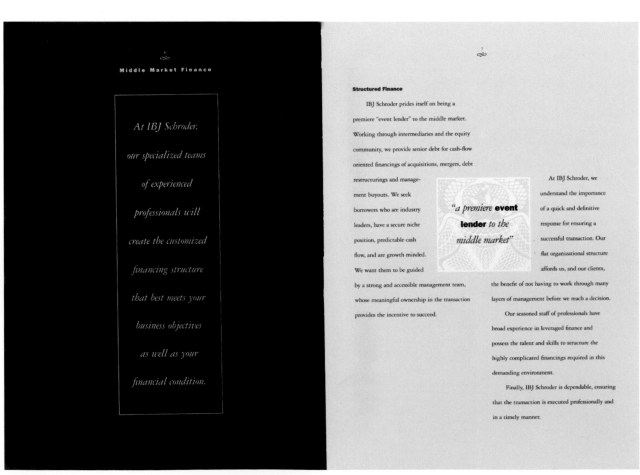

Middle Market Finance

At IBJ Schroder,
our specialized teams
of experienced
professionals will
create the customized
financing structure
that best meets your
business objectives
as well as your
financial condition.

Structured Finance

IBJ Schroder prides itself on being a premiere "event lender" to the middle market. Working through intermediaries and the equity community, we provide senior debt for cash-flow oriented financings of acquisitions, mergers, debt restructurings and management buyouts. We seek borrowers who are industry leaders, have a secure niche position, predictable cash flow, and are growth minded. We want them to be guided by a strong and accessible management team, whose meaningful ownership in the transaction provides the incentive to succeed.

*"a premiere **event lender** to the middle market"*

At IBJ Schroder, we understand the importance of a quick and definitive response for ensuring a successful transaction. Our flat organizational structure affords us, and our clients, the benefit of not having to work through many layers of management before we reach a decision.

Our seasoned staff of professionals have broad experience in leveraged finance and possess the talent and skills to structure the highly complicated financings required in this demanding environment.

Finally, IBJ Schroder is dependable, ensuring that the transaction is executed professionally and in a timely manner.

SBIC — Mezzanine Financing

Through IBJS Capital Corporation, a Small Business Investment Corporation (SBIC), we provide mezzanine financing to seasoned and late-stage middle market companies seeking long-term financing for growth, as well as for acquisitions, buyouts, and restructurings. Typically in the form of a subordinated debt instrument with equity warrants, this type of financing occupies a tier within a client's capital structure between its senior secured debt and its stock.

Working from the perspective of a long-term partner, IBJS Capital Corporation functions as both an experienced lender and a patient investor. In addition to our financial commitment, we invest the time and effort, often as a member of our client's board of directors, to deeply understand our client's business and act as a sounding board to offer insightful and strategic counseling.

> *"IBJS Capital Corporation functions as both an* **experienced** *lender and a* **patient** *investor"*

Our multidimensional role as long-term lender and equity participant underscores our vital interest in our client's long-term success.

As an additional strength, IBJS Capital Corporation's funding is provided by IBJ Schroder itself, a well-established bank with a strong reputation and balance sheet. Thus, the strength and support of our entire institution is lent to the successful outcome of our client's endeavor.

16

Personal Trust and Estate Planning

All too often, individuals create substantial financial security for themselves and their families, only to neglect taking the prudent steps to ensure that the management and distribution of their wealth is handled according to their wishes.

Through Private Client Services, IBJ Schroder's experienced trust professionals help our clients create the right plan to provide for their needs during their lifetime, carry out their instructions after they are gone, and protect their assets from unnecessary estate taxation.

Our Client Advisors will guide clients through the myriad of trust instruments and help in all aspects of the estate-planning process. The bank also offers to serve as trustee to ensure that an estate is properly managed, and/or as executor

> *"***guiding clients*** through the myriad of trust instruments, and helping* **in all aspects** *of the* **estate-planning** *process"*

to fulfill all the estate's obligations and distribute its remaining assets.

IBJ Schroder prides itself on providing assistance beyond the routine settling of estates and management of trusts.

17

Investment Management

IBJ Schroder has been managing its clients' assets since the 1920's, with a consistent record of strong performance.

We credit our long-term success to timely securities selection, a disciplined investment process, an ability to adapt to evolving market conditions and flexibility in meeting our clients' needs.

Our objective is to seek above-average returns while incurring below-average risk, through a value-oriented investment philosophy.

> *"above-average returns through a* **value-oriented** *investment philosophy"*

We aggressively manage the asset mix of our accounts in order to preserve capital in weak markets. Although this strategy has the potential to lag occasionally in rising markets, we believe it is important to limit risk when increased exposure is deemed inappropriate. The net result is that our clients can expect to achieve their investment objectives over each market cycle with below-average volatility.

Each client works with a Client Advisor and a Portfolio Manager to evaluate his or her investment goals, attitudes toward risk, financial and tax circumstances, investment preferences and cash flow requirements, in order to arrive at a customized investment program.

We offer a full range of equity, fixed-income and balanced investment products on an individually managed basis or through an array of mutual funds. Our Managed Allocation Program offers an actively managed, diversified investment program that encompasses a wide range of segments within the investment universe in order to optimize returns for a given level of risk. We also offer products for 401(k)'s and other employee benefit programs.

OBJEKT
PENZINGERSTRASSE 116
1140 WIEN

Creative Firm   **Maireder Grafik-Design**
          Vienna, Austria
Client   *Premium Portfolio Management*

Textured off-white paper of consistent weight makes the cover and text pages of this brochure. Measuring 8-1/2" x 11-5/8", pages are ornamented with muted colors in a very convincing watercolor effect.

Das Objekt

Penzingerstraße 116

Die Penzingerstraße ist eine ruhige Wohnstraße im 14. Wiener Gemeindebezirk, die in der Nähe von Hietzing und Schönbrunn verkehrsgünstig an der Wiener Westeinfahrt liegt. Sowohl die inneren Bezirke, als auch die Westautobahn, sind in wenigen Fahrminuten zu erreichen.

Das Haus Penzingerstraße 116 wurde ca.1920 errichtet und besteht aus Souterrain, Erdgeschoß und zwei Stockwerken, mit einer derzeitigen Nutzfläche von 777 m².

Besonders hervorzuheben ist der dazugehörige Garten, der durch seine Größe von 650 m² als Erholungszone dient.

Durch die Sanierung des Objektes entsteht ein Wohnhaus in ruhiger und trotzdem verkehrsgünstiger Lage; es besteht aus 17 Wohnungen plus 3 Terrassen, einem Büro sowie 4 Garagenplätzen und hat eine Gesamtnutzfläche von 970 m².

Die spezifischen Vorteile:

Im Rahmen des Projektes 14, Penzingerstraße 116, wird jeder Anleger sofort grundbücherlicher Miteigentümer; die Sanierung des Hauses erfolgt auf Basis der vorhandenen Baubeschreibung und gesetzlichen Bestimmungen zum Fixpreis.

Durch die gemeinsame Vermietung wird das persönliche Risiko von Mietausfällen stark reduziert. Als „kleiner Bauherr" realisiert der Anleger neben grundsätzlichen Vorteilen, wie indexierte Mieten und Wertsteigerung, attraktive steuerliche Vorteile.

Die verkehrsgünstige und doch ruhige Lage, der große Garten und die sehr günstigen Mieten sorgen für eine optimale Vermietbarkeit.

Sanierung und Dachgeschoßausbau:

Das Objekt weist eine ausgezeichnete Bausubstanz auf. Die dicken Ziegelmauern sorgen für eine gute Schall- und Wärmeisolierung und für eine baubiologisch gesunde Lebensweise. Folgende bauliche Maßnahmen sind vorgesehen:

- Instandsetzung der bestehenden, freien Wohnungen in Kategorie A
- Dachgeschoßausbau mit 4 Wohnungen plus Terrassen
- Schaffung von 4 Garagenplätzen und einem Büro
- Austausch aller Fenster, Lifteinbau und Sanierung des Stiegenhauses
- zweifärbige Neugestaltung der Fassaden
- Einbau eines Müll- und eines Kinderwagenraumes
- Neugestaltung des Gartens incl. Beleuchtung und Garnitur

Im 650m² großen Garten, der eine wertvolle Ruhe- und Erholungszone darstellt, werden die Wege saniert, 2 Garnituren aufgestellt, und eine Gartenbeleuchtung mit Zeit-und Dämmerungsschalter installiert.

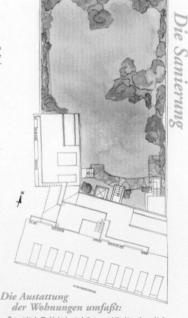

Die Sanierung

Die Austattung der Wohnungen umfaßt:

- Österreichische Tischlerküchen incl. Geräten und Geschirrspüleranschluß (in den Kleinwohnungen Verbau in Schrankelement)
- Heizung und Warmwasseraufbereitung über Gaskombitherme/ Büro (und Top1 Bad und WC) mit Fußbodenheizung
- Böden in Wohnräumen mit hochwertigem Parkett (22mm)
- Bad und WC komplett eingerichtet inclusive Beleuchtung, mit Wanne oder Dusche, WC mechanisch entlüftet, Waschbecken, Spiegel, Waschmaschinenanschluß, im gesamten Sanitärbereich Böden und Wände bis Zargenoberkante verfliest mit farbigem Abschlußriemchen, Sanitärkeramik „Laufen Austrovit Traisen" Fliesenbelag „Marazzi Cita" 15/15, einfärbig weiss
- Beschläge in Messing, Steckdosen und Lichtauslässe weiß
- Gegensprechanlage und Diebstahlsicherungen
- Leerverrohrung für Telefon und Anschluß für Satelliten-TV.

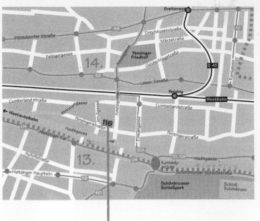

Objekt Penzingerstraße 116

Die Penzingerstraße ist eine ruhige Wohnstraße im 14. Wiener Gemeindebezirk, die in der Nähe von Hietzing und Schönbrunn verkehrsgünstig an der Wiener Westeinfahrt liegt. Sowohl die inneren Bezirke, als auch die Westautobahn, sind in wenigen Fahrminuten zu erreichen.

Anschaffungs- und Sanierungskosten/Finanzierung:

		Finanzierung	
Altgebäude (incl. Nebenkosten, Ausmietung)	8.230.000,-	Eigenmittel: rund 35 %	10.773.000,-
Sanierung (incl. Planung, Konzeption)	17.650.000,-	Fremdmittel: rund 65 %	20.427.000,-
Steuerberatung, Finanzierung, Vertrieb	3.500.000,-		
GrSt, Kredit- u. Eintragungsgebühr	1.820.000,-		
GESAMT	31.200.000,-		31.200.000,-

Umsatzsteuer:

Entsprechend §12 Abs.14 UStG ist die Miteigentümergemeinschaft als umsatzsteuerlicher Unternehmer berechtigt, die ausgewiesene Vorsteuer in Abzug zu bringen.

Finanzierung:

Für den Fremdmittelanteil wurde von einem Zinssatz von 7% und einer Laufzeit von 20 Jahren ausgegangen.

Ein wesentlicher Teil der Finanzierung kann über Bausspardarlehen erfolgen.

Veranlagung in Immobilien:

Die Veranlagung in Immobilien, und dabei speziell in Wohnimmobilien, hat eine lange Tradition. Die besondere Attraktivität dieser Anlageform hat mehrere Gründe:

■ *Sicherheit:*
Wohnen zählt zu den fundamentalsten Bedürfnissen und ist zwar in seiner Form veränderbar, jedoch nicht zu ersetzen. Durch das stete Bevölkerungswachstum erhalten Immobilien auch in wirtschaftlich schwierigen Zeiten ihren Wert. Zusätzliche Sicherheit entsteht durch die Möglichkeit der Eigennutzung in Krisenzeiten.

■ *Ertrag:*
Indexierte Mieten bringen schon nach wenigen Jahren attraktive und regelmäßige Zusatzeinkünfte, die unabhängig von der Entwicklung der Finanzmärkte bzw. der Bonität einzelner Bank- oder Versicherungsinstitute vereinnahmt werden können.

■ *Wertsteigerung:*
Mieterhöhungen bewirken – bei Annahme eines gleichbleibenden Kapitalisierungsfaktors – eine laufende Werterhöhung der Immobilie.
Der Baukostenindex – und damit der Preis neuer Wohnungen – wächst seit Jahrzehnten stärker als der Verbraucherpreisindex.
Ein wesentlicher Teil des Wohnungspreises liegt in den Grundkosten; diese steigen – da Grund und Boden nicht vermehrbar ist – regelmäßig und überdurchschnittlich.
Im Immobilienbereich sind deshalb Wertsteigerungen erzielbar, die deutlich über der Inflationsrate liegen.

Auf Basis dieser Überlegungen stellt die Wohnimmobilie eine sehr attraktive Anlageform dar.
Zur bestmöglichen Absicherung des eigenen Vermögens sollte deshalb ein wesentlicher Teil des eigenen Geldes in Immobilien veranlagt werden.

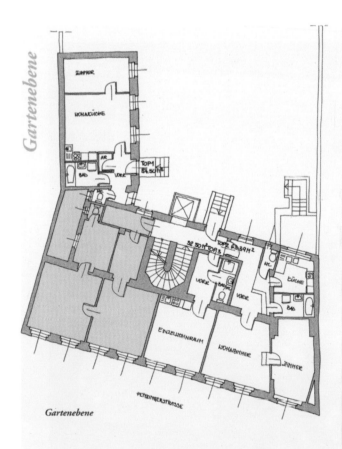

Gartenebene

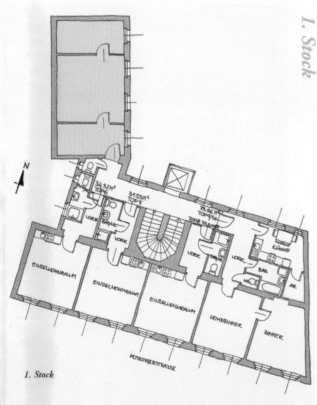

1. Stock

Creative Firm   **Addison**
                New York, New York
Client   *Addison*

Printed on white matte papers with inks and
varnish, this brochure is 9-1/4" x 12-5/8" and
has a glued binding.

153

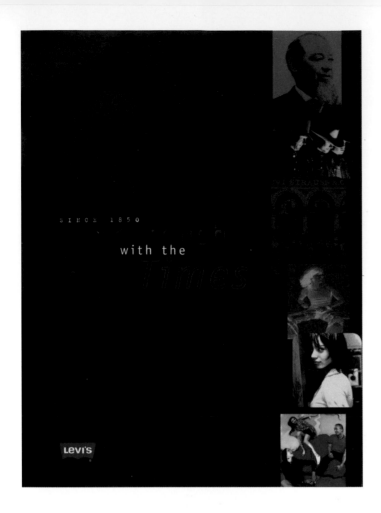

SINCE 1850

with the

Times

LEVI'S

Creative Firm   **White Design**
                   Long Beach, California
Client   *Levi Strauss & Co.*

Two weights of white matte paper are used for the cover and text pages of this 8-3/4" x 11-1/2" brochure. Inside back cover has a vertical pocket. Four-color printing with varnish is found throughout.

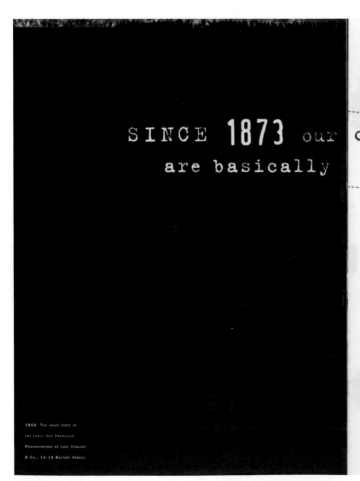

SINCE **1873** our core product jeans **UNCHANGED.** are basically

FOR LEVI STRAUSS & CO., THE 20TH CENTURY begins with two tragedies. Levi Strauss passes away on September 26, 1902. Most of his $6 million estate is left to four nephews and family members. As proof of his legacy of generosity, bequests are also made to various charities.

The San Francisco Board of Trade pronounces: "...the great causes of education and charity have...suffered a signal loss in the death of Mr. Strauss...whose numberless...acts of charity in which neither race nor creed were recognized, exemplified his broad and generous love for and sympathy with humanity."

IN 1906, A MASSIVE EARTHQUAKE AND FIRE destroy Levi Strauss & Co. factories, and most of San Francisco. The company rebuilds. Levi's nephews — the Stern brothers — make plans for a new factory at 250 Valencia Street.

THE COMPANY EXPANDS. In 1912, "Koveralls," a one-piece children's playsuit, becomes the company's first product sold nationally. Waist overalls are still only sold in the West.

SIGMUND STERN ASKS his son-in-law, Walter Haas, to join the company in 1919. Because of slow sales, he's challenged to turn the company around in two years. Armed with a meager annual advertising budget of $25,000 to make the Levi's® brand a household name, he triumphs.

OVER THE NEXT THREE DECADES, the mystique of Levi's® jeans grows. Easterners visiting dude ranches in the 1930s purchase authentic western wear, giving our clothing its first national exposure. Women discover a new wardrobe item.

1866 THE SALES STAFF AT THE EARLY SAN FRANCISCO HEADQUARTERS OF LEVI STRAUSS & CO., 14-16 BATTERY STREET.

top to bottom: 1829 LEVI (LEVI) STRAUSS IS BORN IN BAVARIA. MOVES TO AMERICA IN 1847. 1850 JONAS AND LOUIS STRAUSS TEACH THEIR HALF-BROTHER, LEVI, THE DRY GOODS BUSINESS IN NEW YORK. 1853 LEVI ARRIVED IN SAN FRANCISCO DURING THE GOLD RUSH. 1872 JACOB DAVIS, A RENO, NEVADA TAILOR, WRITES LEVI, SUGGESTING A PROCESS TO RIVET POCKET CORNERS. 1873 PATENTS ARE GRANTED FOR THE RIVETS. A FACTORY IN S.F. IS BUILT TO PRODUCE DENIM COPPER-RIVETED CLOTHING, KNOWN AS "WAIST OVERALLS."

1873

154

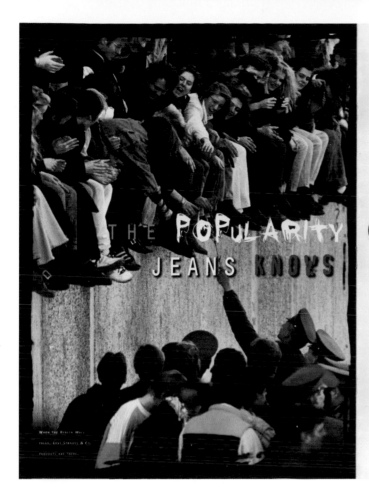

THE **POPULARITY** OF LEVI'S®
JEANS KNOWS NO BOUNDARIES.

People have worn Levi Strauss & Co. products in the California gold mines, through two World Wars, from building the Golden Gate Bridge to tearing down the Berlin Wall, in small towns, in vast cities, to school, to the office, to the White House, to Red Square to the Blue Danube.

OUR PRODUCTS ARE THE CLOTHING OF CHOICE, manufactured by the employer of choice, in a workplace that is productive, safe, challenging, rewarding and fun. Being the employer of choice is a company-wide goal with great challenges, and even greater rewards.

It uses the skills, talents and ideas of all of our employees to anticipate — and to lead — change.

EVERY GARMENT WE MAKE is still created with the original values and aspirations Levi Strauss shared with generations of family and employees in the 1850s. These include: teamwork and trust, a diversity in the workforce at all levels, leadership by recognition, ethical management practices, an environment of shared communications and corporate empowerment.

Social RESPONSIBILITIES.

Our company's future will be built on the foundation of social and corporate responsibilities first instituted by Levi Strauss himself... from his creation of student scholarships at the University of California, Berkeley, in the 1890s to the opening of racially-integrated company factories in the 1940s to the establishment of a Global Environmental Council in the early 1990s.

THE LEVI STRAUSS FOUNDATION — and Levi Strauss & Co. — generously channel our resources to communities where we work and live. We donate more than $20 million annually in charitable gifts to community organizations in nearly 40 countries.

We stand behind some of the most controversial social issues because we recognize that they are important to the quality of community life. We sponsor education programs and policies on AIDS, support anti-racism and social justice initiatives, and promote economic empowerment for the poor and disenfranchised.

WE EMPOWER EACH EMPLOYEE to make a difference. Our Community Involvement Teams (C.I.T.) support employee volunteerism and local community services. Our first C.I.T. began in 1968, and now there are over 100 teams of employee volunteers around the world. The Red Tab Foundation assists employees and their families faced with unexpected financial burdens. In 1989, we inaugurated an employee program to help immigrants working in our American facilities to become United States citizens. In 1992, we developed our Global Sourcing and Operating Guidelines, a code of conduct to ensure that our products are manufactured in a responsible way. We were the first company in any industry to establish and rigorously enforce such a far-reaching code with business partners around the world.

Today our commitment to corporate social responsibility is a common thread woven throughout the history of our global organization.

Corporate VALUES.

RACE FOR THE CURE

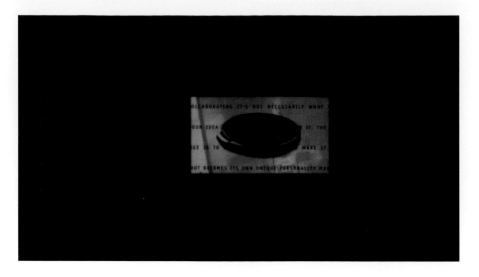

Creative Firm   **Scott Brown Design**
                       Redwood City, California
Client   *Miles Keep*

Brochure opens from the left. Cover is textured,
maroon, heavyweight paper. Double-thick front
cover with die cut displays icon printed on acetate.
Inside, slick, white, glossy paper is used for text
pages, and is accented by front and back sheets
of printed vellum. Brochure measures 11-1/4" x
6-1/4".

415.969.6701

MILES KEEP PHOTOGRAPHY

415.969.6701

MILES KEEP PHOTOGRAPHY

415.969.6701

MILES KEEP PHOTOGRAPHY

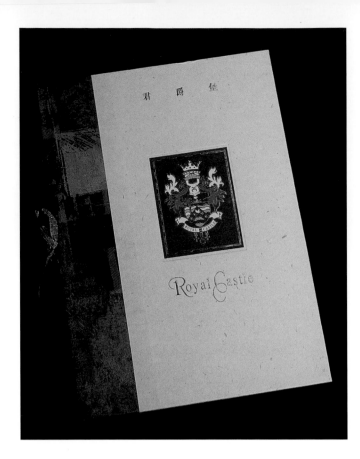

Creative Firm   **KINGGRAPHIC**
                         Hong Kong, China
Client   *Full Seas Group*

This book-brochure comes in a gold foil stamped, card case with accompanying staple-bound brochure. Spine of book is covered with a silk jacquard, while other cover elements include debossing, and gold foil stamping. Inner pages are printed on a white matte textured stock. Though stapled together, pages are held in place with a metallic gold ribbon which ties to the outside of the book. Measurement is 8-1/2" x 12".

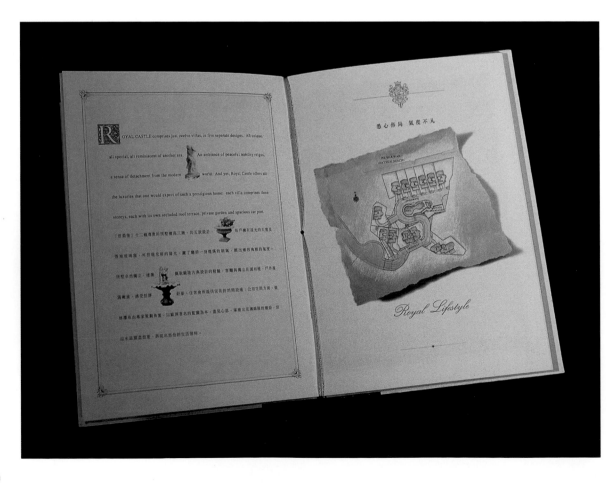

ELEMENTS OF JOB PARILUX J⬦B

chihuly

THE FIRE

Creative Firm **Design One**
San Francisco, California
Client *Job Parilux*

Job Parilux, a recycled, and acid- and chlorine-free paper, is the choice for this brochure. Gloss 74 lb. is used for text pages; gloss 111 lb. cover makes the cover. Four-color process and gloss varnish are employed throughout the brochure with the addition of an aqueous coating on the cover. Total brochure measures 9" x 12". Inside back cover has a curved-edge flap. Center spread folds out completely from both sides.

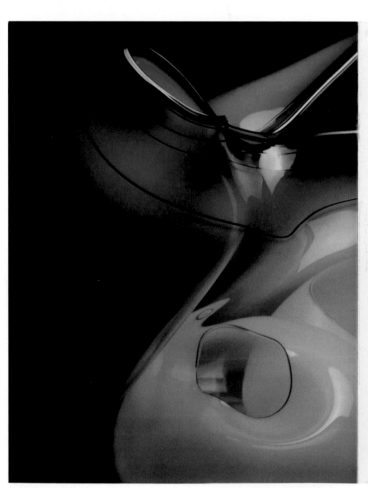

DALE CHIHULY

SINCE THE 1960s DALE CHIHULY HAS PRODUCED
A REMARKABLE PROFUSION OF INTERNATIONALLY
ACCLAIMED MASTERWORKS. IN HIS STUDIO, THE
BOATHOUSE ON SEATTLE'S LAKE UNION, CHIHULY
CREATES MASTERPIECES WITH THE ASSISTANCE OF
A TEAM OF GLASSWORKERS, GIVING SHAPE TO HIS
CONTINUALLY EVOLVING VISIONS.

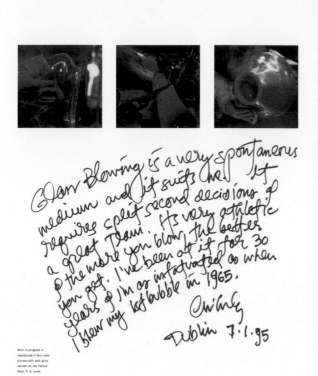

Glass Blowing is a very spontaneous medium and it suits me. It requires split second decisions & a great team. It's very athletic & the more you blow the better you get. I've been at it for 30 years & I'm as infatuated as when I blew my 1st bubble in 1965.

Chihuly

Dublin 7·1·95

Work in progress is reproduced in four-color process with spot gloss varnish on Job Parilux Gloss 74 lb. cover.

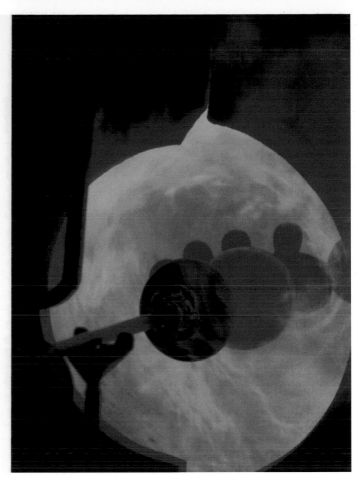

I love the Putti!

Chihuly

Erbium Chandelier with Gilded Putti, 34 x 54 x 54 inches, 1993.

Reproduction in four-color process with magenta and black touch-plates and gloss varnish on Job Parilux Gloss 74 lb. cover.

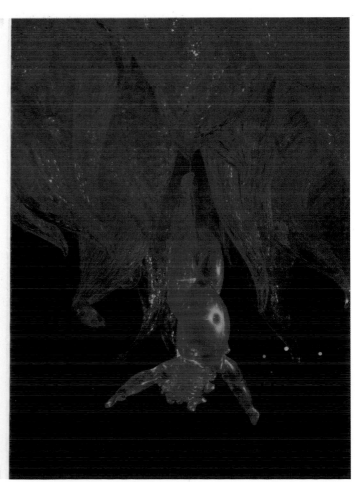

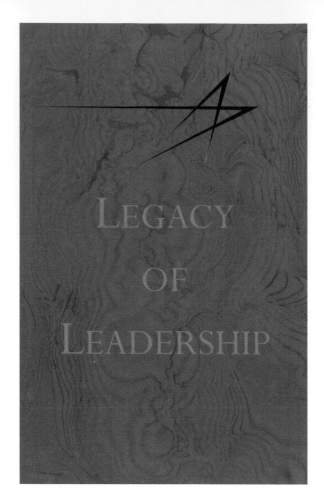

LEGACY

OF

LEADERSHIP

Creative Firm **Taylor & Ives Incorporated**
New York, New York
Client *Lockheed Martin Corporation*

Fibered, sage green paper, and white matte stock make
up the text pages of this 7-1/2" x 12" brochure with a
glued binding. Cover is printed with a marble "texture"
and is gold foil stamped.

SIGNIFICANT

EVENTS AND

ACCOMPLISHMENTS

OF THE HERITAGE

LOCKHEED

MARTIN

COMPANIES

1909

GLENN L. MARTIN'S FIRST
FLIGHT

*On August 1, 1909 aviation pio-
neer Glenn L. Martin fulfills a
dream by flying his silk and
bamboo aircraft for the first time
— over a distance of 100 feet
and no more than eight feet off
the ground. Two years later,
The Martin Company is established. Donald Douglas and
James McDonnell, who went on
to establish their own companies, earlier joined Martin.*

5

1969

RIGHT ON TARGET

A major advance in the development of modern precision weaponry is pioneered in 1969 by Ford Aerospace with the introduction of the Pave Knife laser target designator. Pave Knife becomes the first electro-optical targeting system used by the U.S. Air Force and U.S. Navy in actual combat, during the conflict in Vietnam. It leads to later precision laser-guided weapons systems such as Pave Tack and NITE Hawk.

1970

EARS BENEATH THE SEA

In a major breakthrough, IBM Federal Systems-Manassas develop the first digital sonar capability for the U.S. Navy's AN/BQQ5 program in 1970. Three years later the company develops and produces the Navy's first Standard Acoustic Signal Processor. Both greatly enhance the nation's undersea warfare capability.

1969

ONE GIANT LEAP

When Neil Armstrong makes history as the first man on the Moon in 1969, his 'Eagle' Lunar Excursion Module was equipped with pulsed integrating pendulum accelerometers from Sperry. Subsequent Moon landings involve contributions from other heritage companies including Martin (zero-reaction tools first used in 1971 to drill holes in the lunar surface), and Goodyear Aerospace (radar recorder for lunar sounder aboard Apollo 17).

1996

THE SHAPE OF THINGS TO FLY

Vice President Al Gore and NASA Administrator Dan Goldin announce in 1996 the selection of a Lockheed Martin team as winner of the X-33 single-stage-to-orbit reusable launch vehicle program. Lockheed Martin's VentureStar™ is selected because of a variety of technological innovations including an aerodynamically efficient lifting body configuration, linear aerospike engines that adjust themselves to perform *with maximum efficiency at all altitudes, and the extensive use of high-strength, low-weight composite materials. Lockheed Martin also proposes a unique business plan to transition VentureStar from development to a financially viable operational phase after the turn of the century.*

COLLIER TROPHY PRESENTATIONS INVOLVING HERITAGE LOCKHEED MARTIN COMPANIES

1914

Elmer A. Sperry - For gyroscopic control

1916

Elmer A. Sperry - For Sperry drift site

1932

Glenn L. Martin - For development of a high-speed weight-carrying airplane

1936

Pan American Airways for the establishment of the trans-Pacific airplane and the successful execution of extended overwater navigation in the regular operation thereof

1937

U.S. Army Air Corps for developing, equipping and flying the first successful pressure cabin airplane, the XC-35

1958

The United States Air Force and Industry Team Responsible for the F-104 Interceptor; Clarence L. "Kelly" Johnson of Lockheed Aircraft Corporation for the design of the airframe; Neil Burgess and Gerhard Neumann of the Flight Propulsion Division, General Electric

Company, for development of the J-79 turbo jet engines; Major Howard C. Johnson, USAF, for establishing a world land plane altitude record of 91,243 feet, and Captain Walter W. Irwin, USAF, for establishing a world straightaway speed record of 1,404.09 miles per hour

1959

The United States Air Force, The Convair Division of General Dynamics Corporation and Space Technology Laboratories, Inc., for developing, testing, producing and putting into operation the Atlas, America's first intercontinental ballistic missile so vital to the security and space exploration needs of the United States and the free world

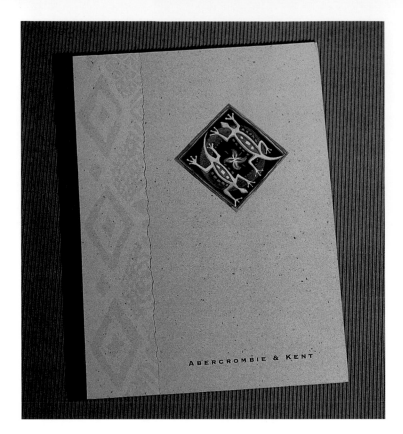

Creative Firm   **DHI (Designs Horizons Intl.)**
                      Chicago, Illinois
Client   *Abercrombie + Kent*

Flap (with "deckle"-cut edge) from back cover
wraps around to front. Saddle-stitched
binding is covered with a strip of woven book
tape. Smooth paper is printed with inks and
varnish. Middle spread offers foldout, while
entire piece measures 9-1/4" x 11-7/8".

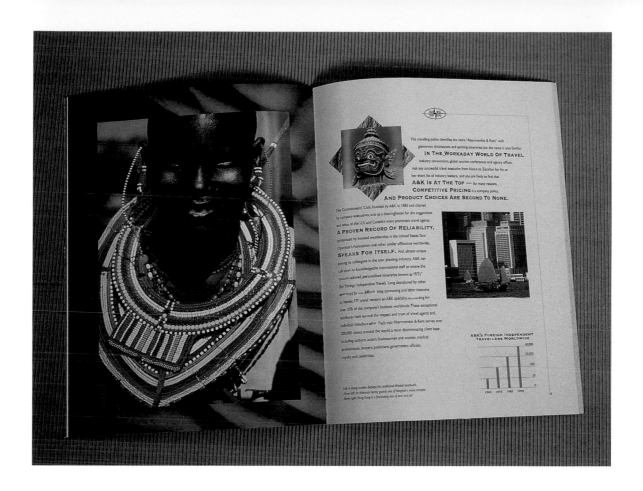

Full Line Collection

aiwa

Creative Firm   **Paganucci Design, Inc.**
New York, New York
Client   *AIWA*

Cover is a lined-textured, white dull stock. Text pages of 8-1/2" x 11" brochure are white glossy.

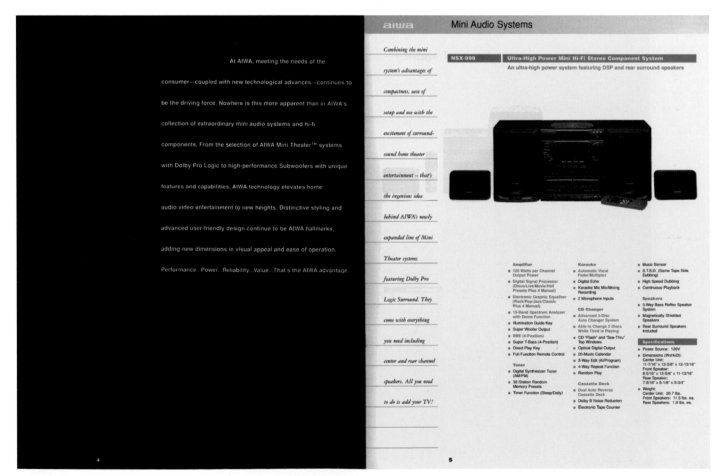

At AIWA, meeting the needs of the consumer—coupled with new technological advances—continues to be the driving force. Nowhere is this more apparent than in AIWA's collection of extraordinary mini audio systems and hi-fi components. From the selection of AIWA Mini Theater™ systems with Dolby Pro Logic to high-performance Subwoofers with unique features and capabilities, AIWA technology elevates home audio video entertainment to new heights. Distinctive styling and advanced user-friendly design continue to be AIWA hallmarks, adding new dimensions in visual appeal and ease of operation.

Performance...Power...Reliability...Value...That's the AIWA advantage.

Combining the mini system's advantages of compactness, ease of setup and use with the excitement of surround-sound home theater entertainment — that's the ingenious idea behind AIWA's newly expanded line of Mini Theater systems featuring Dolby Pro Logic Surround. They come with everything you need including center and rear channel speakers. All you need to do is add your TV!

aiwa   Mini Audio Systems

NSX-999   **Ultra-High Power Mini Hi-Fi Stereo Component System**
An ultra-high power system featuring DSP and rear surround speakers

Amplifier
- 120 Watts per Channel Output Power
- Digital Signal Processor (Disco/Live/Movie/Hall Presets Plus 4 Manual)
- Electronic Graphic Equalizer (Rock/Pop/Jazz/Classic Plus 4 Manual)
- 15-Band Spectrum Analyzer with Demo Function
- Illumination Guide Key
- Super Woofer Output
- BBE (4-Position)
- Super T-Bass (4-Position)
- Direct Play Key
- Full Function Remote Control

Tuner
- Digital Synthesizer Tuner (AM/FM)
- 32-Station Random Memory Presets
- Timer Function (Sleep/Daily)

Karaoke
- Automatic Vocal Fader/Multiplex
- Digital Echo
- Karaoke Mic Mix/Mixing Recording
- 2 Microphone Inputs

CD Changer
- Advanced 3-Disc Auto Changer System
- Able to Change 2 Discs While Third is Playing
- CD "Flash" and "See-Thru" Top Windows
- Optical Digital Output
- 20-Music Calendar
- 2-Way Edit (All/Program)
- 4-Way Repeat Function
- Random Play

Cassette Deck
- Dual Auto Reverse Cassette Deck
- Dolby B Noise Reduction
- Electronic Tape Counter

- Music Sensor
- S.T.S.D. (Same Tape Side Dubbing)
- High Speed Dubbing
- Continuous Playback

Speakers
- 3-Way Bass Reflex Speaker System
- Magnetically Shielded Speakers
- Rear Surround Speakers Included

Specifications
- Power Source: 120V
- Dimensions (WxHxD):
Center Unit:
11-7/16" x 12-5/8" x 12-13/16"
Front Speaker:
8-5/16" x 12-5/8" x 11-13/16"
Rear Speaker:
7-5/16" x 5-1/8" x 5-3/4"
- Weight:
Center Unit: 20.7 lbs.
Front Speakers: 11.5 lbs. ea.
Rear Speakers: 1.8 lbs. ea.

4

5

Meticulously engineered

to deliver unmatched

performance and

reliability, AIWA

portable CD players are

the choice of discerning

CD enthusiasts the

world over. They

combine advanced

technology with

sophisticated slimline

styling to ensure superb

sound quality, timeless

good looks, and

effortless portability.

Add a Car Kit,

which includes

easy-to-use DC and

cassette adaptors.

XP-750 | **Portable CD Player with 10-Second E.A.S.S.**

E.A.S.S. with 10-second memory provides the ultimate in resistance to shock

- E.A.S.S. (Electronic Anti-Shock System) with 10 Seconds Memory
- Rechargeable (with the purchase of Ni-Cd Rechargeable Battery)
- Heat-Resistant for In-Car and Outdoor Use
- 3-Point Battery Life LED Indicator
- Back-Lit LCD Display
- DSL—AIWA's Dynamic Super Linear Bass
- 24-Selection Random Program Memory
- Slim Design
- 2-Way Repeat Play
- Resume Play
- 1-Bit Dual D/A Converter
- Available with Car Kit (DC and Cassette Adaptor)

Specifications
- Power Source: AC: through AC Adaptor DC: 3V ("AA" x 2)
- Dimensions (WxHxD): 5-1/8" x 6" x 1-1/4"
- Weight: 8.8 oz.

XP-750 includes Car Kit

XP-520 | **Portable CD Player with E.A.S.S.**

E.A.S.S. with 3-second memory improves shock resistance for enhanced portability

- E.A.S.S. (Electronic Anti-Shock System) with 3-Second Memory
- Rechargeable (with the purchase of Ni-Cd Rechargeable Battery)
- Heat-Resistant for In-Car and Outdoor Use
- 3-Point Battery Life LED Indicator
- DSL—AIWA's Dynamic Super Linear Bass
- 24-Selection Random Program Memory
- 2-Way Repeat Play (One/All)
- Resume Play
- 1-Bit Dual D/A Converter
- Available with Car Kit (DC and Cassette Adaptor)

Specifications
- Power Source: AC: through AC Adaptor DC: 3V ("AA" x 2)
- Dimensions (WxHxD): 5-1/3" x 6-1/2" x 1-1/2"
- Weight: 9.6 oz.

XP-529 includes Car Kit   XP-521 in white

20

Models with AIWA's

E.A.S.S. (Electronic

Anti-Shock System)

deliver music on the go

without annoying

skips and interruptions.

DSL (Dynamic Super

Linear Bass) provides

extended, authoritative

bass reproduction.

Models with built-in

high-performance

Digital Synthesizer

AM/FM Tuner

add the ability to

enjoy broadcast

programming.

XP-R800 | **Portable CD Player with Digital Tuner and E.A.S.S.**

Unsurpassed CD reproduction with the added versatility of a built-in digital synthesizer AM/FM tuner

- Digital Synthesizer Tuner (AM/FM)
- E.A.S.S.—Electronic Anti-Shock System with 3-Seconds Memory)
- 30-Station Random Memory Presets
- Rechargeable (with purchase of AIWA's Ni-MH Rechargeable Battery)
- Heat Resistant for In-Car and Outdoor Use
- 3-Point Battery Life LED Indicator
- 24-Selection Random Program Memory
- 2-Way Repeat Play (One/All)
- 1-Bit Dual D/A Converter

Specifications
- Power Source: AC: through AC Adaptor DC: 3V ("AA" x 2)
- Dimensions (WxHxD): 5-5/16" x 1-1/4" x 16-5/16"
- Weight (w/o Batteries): 10.6 oz.

XP-R650 | **Portable CD Player with Digital Tuner**

A superb portable CD player with built-in precision digital synthesizer AM/FM tuner

- Digital Synthesizer Tuner (AM/FM)
- 30-Station Random Preset Memory
- Rechargeable (with the purchase of Ni-Cd Rechargeable Battery)
- Heat-Resistant for In-Car and Outdoor Use
- Auto Tuning
- 3-Point Battery Life LED Indicator
- DSL—AIWA's Dynamic Super Linear Bass
- 24-Selection Random Program Memory
- 2-Way Repeat Play (One/All)
- Resume Play
- 1-Bit Dual D/A Converter

Specifications
- Power Source: AC: through AC Adaptor DC: 3V ("AA" x 2)
- Dimensions (WxHxD): 5-1/3" x 6-1/2" x 1-1/2"
- Weight: 9.8 oz.

21

HP-V041 | **In-Ear Type Headphones**

Excellent cost/performance in an in-ear model, featuring Pipe-Phone technology

- Acoustic Pipe for Deep Bass Sound
- 5/8" (15mm) Driver Units
- Tangle Resistant OFC Cord
- L-Shaped Stereo Mini-Plug
- 10Hz-25kHz Frequency Response

AIWA cordless

headphones deliver the

ultimate in freedom.

They also provide

excellent sound quality

thanks to advanced

AIWA design and

engineering.

HP-WA301 | **Cordless Headphone System**

Extended listening time, using two alkaline "AA" batteries for up to 110 hours of operation

- High Grade Infra-Red System for High Quality, Free-Style Listening
- Large 1-3/16" (30mm) Driver Units
- One-Sided Dual Control Volume Switch
- Noise Suppressing Muting System
- Easy Connection to AV Components
- Compact Transmitter with Auto Power On/Off Circuit
- 20Hz-20kHz Frequency Response

62

Whether for

general-purpose

recording, karaoke,

entertainment or

professional recording,

count on AIWA

microphones to deliver

the performance

and features you need.

DM-H100 | **Uni-Directional Microphone**

An affordable high-quality vocal microphone, excellent for karaoke use

- Uni-Directional Pick-Up Pattern
- Built-In On/Off Switch
- Stereo Mini-Plug
- Standard Plug Adapter
- 50Hz-15kHz Frequency Response
- Cord Length: 9' 10"

63

The Codec Connection

DIALOG4®

Creative Firm   **swf+f Büros für Werbung**
                 Stuttgart, Germany
Client   *Dialog4 System Engineering GmbH*

Binding is stapled with extending staples so brochure can be stored in a notebook. White dull paper is used for this 8-1/4" x 11-5/8" brochure.

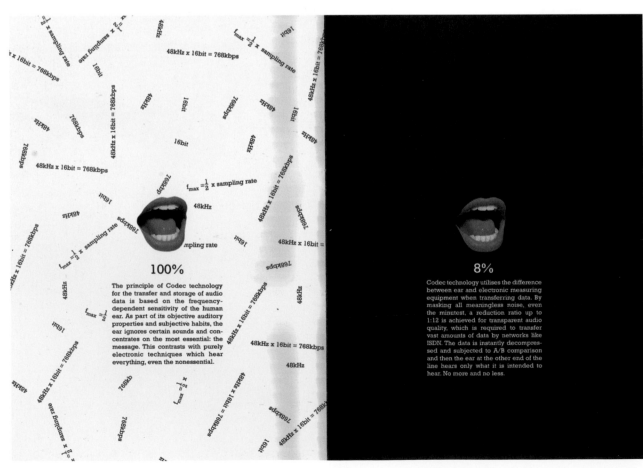

100%

The principle of Codec technology for the transfer and storage of audio data is based on the frequency-dependent sensitivity of the human ear. As part of its objective auditory properties and subjective habits, the ear ignores certain sounds and concentrates on the most essential: the message. This contrasts with purely electronic techniques which hear everything, even the nonessential.

8%

Codec technology utilises the difference between ear and electronic measuring equipment when transferring data. By masking all meaningless noise, even the minutest, a reduction ratio up to 1:12 is achieved for transparent audio quality, which is required to transfer vast amounts of data by networks like ISDN. The data is instantly decompressed and subjected to A/B comparison and then the ear at the other end of the line hears only what it is intended to hear. No more and no less.

Switch

DAB

Layer III

MUSICAM

G.722

G.711

J.52

You pay

transmission cost in proportion to quality.

Six B-channels Layer II cost more, one B-channel Layer III that

much less.

Creative Firm   **Dunn and Rice Design**
                  Rochester, New York
Client   *Canfield & Tack, Inc.*

Four-color process, match colors, metallic inks, and various varnishes were used in the printing of this 9" x 12" brochure. Colored matte, and white gloss papers were also chosen.

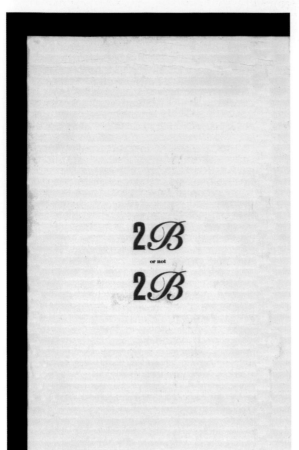

Creative Firm   **Paganucci Design, Inc.**
New York, New York
Client   *Merrill Lynch*

Embossed, and gold foil stamped case of white glossy stock comprises a holder for this brochure. Cover is also white glossy with embossed, gold foil stamping. Text pages are alternately a fibered, taupe stock, and white glossy paper. Fibered paper pages are cut smaller than brochure's overall measurement of 8-1/2" x 14".

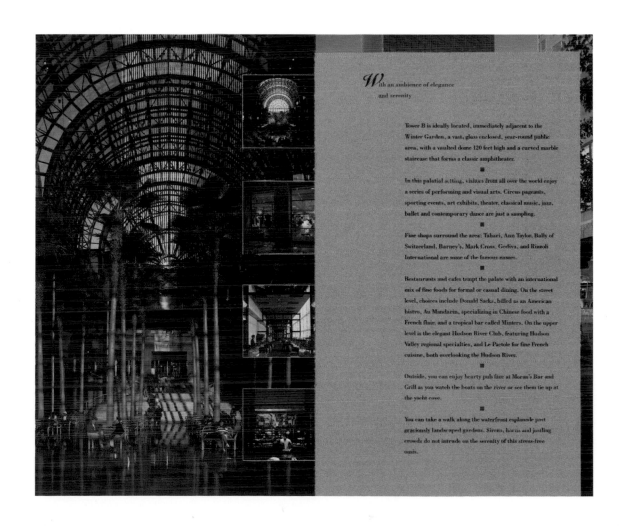

An office and retail complex of unprecedented quality

Between the World Trade Center and the New York Harbor stands the finest office complex in New York City—the World Financial Center—a truly extraordinary business environment, and the only office property with direct access to the water's edge.

Designed by architect Cesar Pelli on 14 landscaped acres, the Center's four granite and glass towers are set in surroundings that include a waterside plaza, walkways, gardens, waterfalls and a cove for ocean-going yachts. Of the 8 million square feet of commercial space, 280,000 are devoted to fine shops, cafes and restaurants. The complex stands as the centerpiece of Battery Park City, a 92-acre commercial and residential community with 30,000 dwelling units and landscaped parks, acclaimed as a masterpiece of urban planning and design.

In Two World Financial Center (Tower B), at the center of the complex, a total of 420,000 square feet of world class office space is available for lease on six floors of 50,000 and three floors of 40,000 square feet, all with breathtaking views of river, harbor, city, sun and sky.

With an ambience of elegance and serenity

Tower B is ideally located, immediately adjacent to the Winter Garden, a vast, glass enclosed, year-round public area, with a vaulted dome 120 feet high and a curved marble staircase that forms a classic amphitheater.

In this palatial setting, visitors from all over the world enjoy a series of performing and visual arts. Circus pageants, sporting events, art exhibits, theater, classical music, jazz, ballet and contemporary dance are just a sampling.

Fine shops surround the area: Tahari, Ann Taylor, Bally of Switzerland, Barney's, Mark Cross, Godiva, and Rizzoli International are some of the famous names.

Restaurants and cafes tempt the palate with an international mix of fine foods for formal or casual dining. On the street level, choices include Donald Sacks, billed as an American bistro, Au Mandarin, specializing in Chinese food with a French flair, and a tropical bar called Minters. On the upper level is the elegant Hudson River Club, featuring Hudson Valley regional specialties, and Le Pactole for fine French cuisine, both overlooking the Hudson River.

Outside, you can enjoy hearty pub fare at Moran's Bar and Grill as you watch the boats on the river or see them tie up at the yacht cove.

You can take a walk along the waterfront esplanade past graciously landscaped gardens. Sirens, horns and jostling crowds do not intrude on the serenity of this stress-free oasis.

173

*A*ccessible to everything and from everywhere

Convenience and accessibility are unmatched. By design, the World Financial Center is easy to reach by subway, bus, train, helicopter, car or ferry.

All the buildings of the Center are connected by a system of interior walkways. Two World Financial Center leads directly to an enclosed pedestrian bridge that protects commuters from the elements on the short walk to the World Trade Center, a major stop on the New York subway and PATH rail systems. Fifteen subway lines are within a seven-block radius, and as many as 4,500 garage parking spaces are immediately available or close by. A conveniently located ferry slip simplifies travel between Battery Park City and Hoboken, New Jersey; all three major metropolitan airports are easily accessible, and a heliport is not far away.

The pedestrian bridges also provide easy access to the stock exchanges, the financial, insurance and court districts and City Hall. For the convenience of visitors, luxury hotels like the Vista and Marriott are across the street.

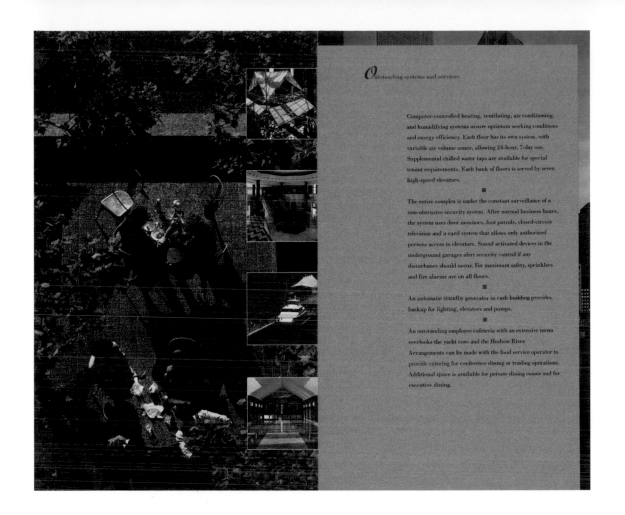

Outstanding systems and services

Computer-controlled heating, ventilating, air conditioning, and humidifying systems assure optimum working conditions and energy efficiency. Each floor has its own system, with variable air volume zones, allowing 24-hour, 7-day use. Supplemental chilled water taps are available for special tenant requirements. Each bank of floors is served by seven high-speed elevators.

The entire complex is under the constant surveillance of a non-obtrusive security system. After normal business hours, the system uses door monitors, foot patrols, closed-circuit television and a card system that allows only authorized persons access to elevators. Sound activated devices in the underground garages alert security control if any disturbance should occur. For maximum safety, sprinklers and fire alarms are on all floors.

An automatic standby generator in each building provides backup for lighting, elevators and pumps.

An outstanding employee cafeteria with an extensive menu overlooks the yacht cove and the Hudson River. Arrangements can be made with the food service operator to provide catering for conference dining or trading operations. Additional space is available for private dining rooms and for executive dining.

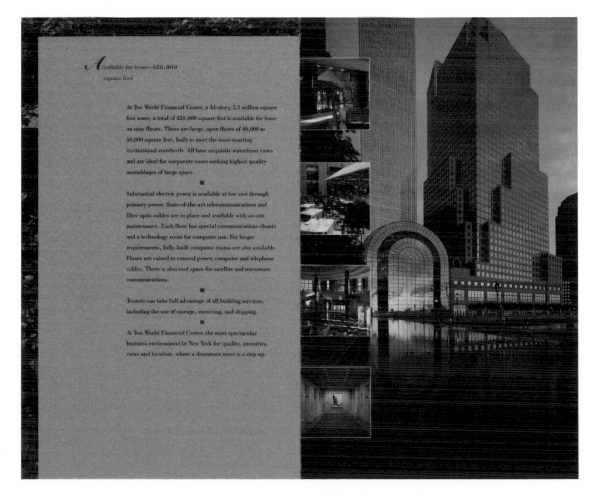

Available for lease—420,000 square feet

At Two World Financial Center, a 44-story, 2.3 million square foot tower, a total of 420,000 square feet is available for lease on nine floors. These are large, open floors of 40,000 to 50,000 square feet, built to meet the most exacting institutional standards. All have exquisite waterfront views and are ideal for corporate users seeking highest quality assemblages of large space.

Substantial electric power is available at low cost through primary power. State-of-the-art telecommunications and fiber optic cables are in place and available with on-site maintenance. Each floor has special communications closets and a technology room for computer use. For larger requirements, fully-built computer rooms are also available. Floors are raised to conceal power, computer and telephone cables. There is also roof space for satellite and microwave communications.

Tenants can take full advantage of all building services, including the use of storage, receiving, and shipping.

At Two World Financial Center, the most spectacular business environment in New York for quality, amenities, views and location—where a downtown move is a step up.

Creative Firm **Keiler & Company**
Farmer, Connecticut
Client *Deloitte & Touche*

Book-brochure comes in a heavy board case reminiscent of Time-Life® record cases. Inside, it measures 11-7/8" x 11-3/4". Brochure cover is fabric covered. It is also blind debossed, and debossed and printed. Gray textured endpapers contrast white semigloss text sheets.

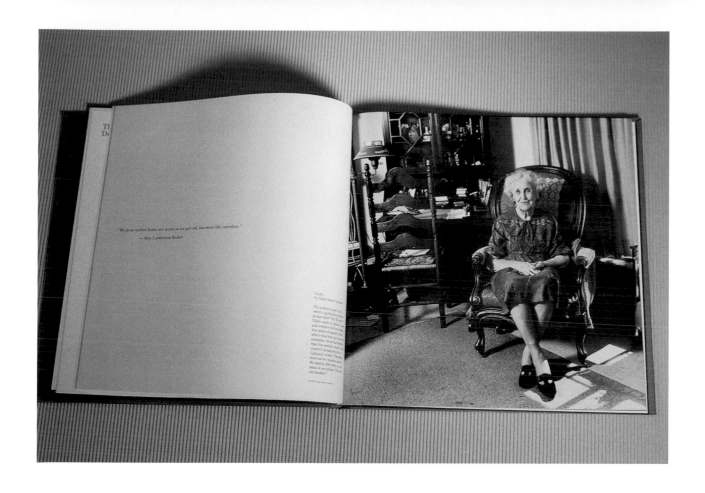

"We grow neither better nor worse as we get old, but more like ourselves."
— May Lamberton Becker

"Age does not make us childish, as they say. It only finds us true children still."
—Johann Wolfgang von Goethe, Faust

Girolamo, 1995
by Frank Marchese

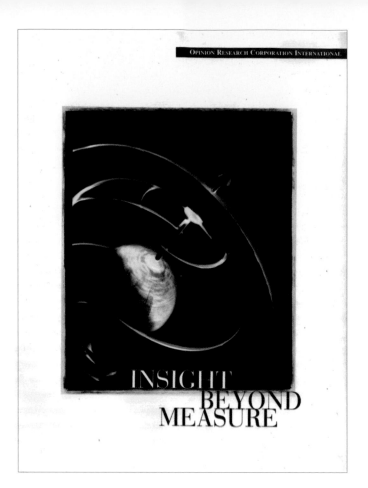

INSIGHT
BEYOND
MEASURE

Creative Firm   **Paganucci Design, Inc.**
                 New York, New York
Client   *Opinion Research*

Brochure uses white matte papers of differing thicknesses for the cover and interior, respectively. Back inside cover has a vertical pocket. Varnish, in addition to regular inks, were integral in the printing of this 8-5/8" x 11-1/2" brochure.

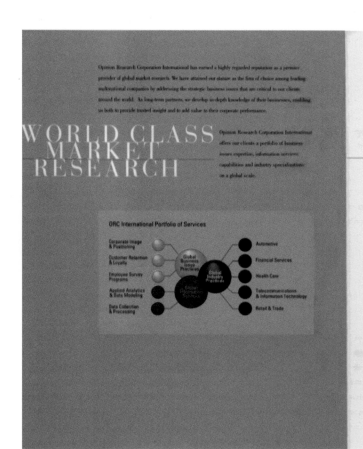

Encouraging and strengthening client relationships—developing long-term customer loyalty— are critical, bottom-line considerations in today's competitive marketplace. Loyal customers reduce a company's overall business costs as key customers make recurrent purchases, buy additional products and services, and refer new business opportunities.

Komatsu, the Japanese-based manufacturer of heavy construction and mining equipment, sells its products to customers through an independent distribution network. To support its dealer channel in North America, the company sought to establish a proactive quality assurance program to obtain detailed customer feedback, measure loyalty and satisfaction, and provide customer-based information on pre- and post-purchase service.

For the Komatsu America subsidiary, ORC International launched the exclusive PULSE program in May 1995. PULSE enables Komatsu and its distributors to: evaluate multiple drivers of customer loyalty; access detailed market-based information and determine where to take action; listen— literally—to the voice of their customers; respond immediately to customer concerns; evaluate new product success; and provide benchmarks of performance.

"Through the PULSE program, ORC International has provided Komatsu with a problem-solving and management tool that can change the whole organization, and help in developing stronger relationships with our customers." —Jenkins Davis, Komatsu

KOMATSU

Because the program's goal is to develop long-term relationships with customers, we conduct telephone interviews with the purchase decision-makers at one-, six-, and 30-month intervals after delivery of a new machine and with maintenance supervisors annually for three years after purchase. Downloaded into a dedicated computer database, the information collected from the conversations forms the core of an ongoing database to monitor and analyze customer responses.

As part of PULSE, we activate a special "alert" system during interviews to record (with the respondent's consent) the customer's concerns, queries or interest in a new purchase. We then communicate a summary of the remarks to the relevant distributor and Komatsu regional office, along with a computer access code to listen to the recording in the customer's own voice.

The market intelligence gained through PULSE reinforces long-term relationships among Komatsu, its dealers and customers. We help our client retain loyal customers by enabling Komatsu and its distributors to focus their businesses on the needs of their customers — to create customers for life.

From left:
Jenkins Davis,
Komatsu; Ed Short,
ORC International;
Linda Shen,
ORC International.

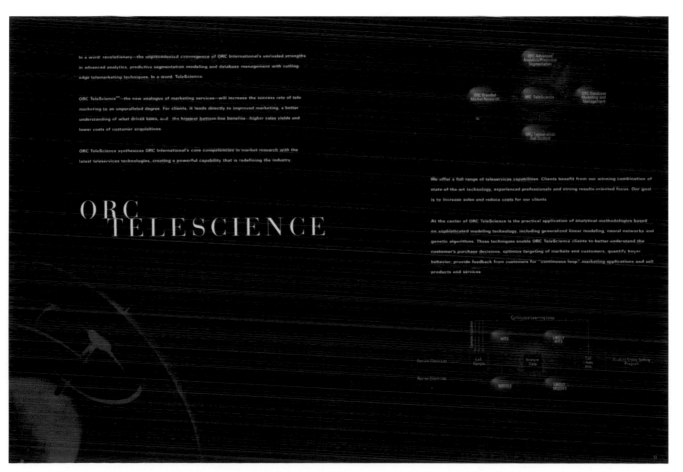

In a word: revolutionary—the unprecedented convergence of ORC International's unrivaled strengths in advanced analytics, predictive segmentation modeling and database management with cutting edge telemarketing techniques. In a word: TeleScience.

ORC TeleScience™—the new analogue of marketing services—will increase the success rate of telemarketing to an unparalleled degree. For clients, it leads directly to improved marketing, a better understanding of what drives sales, and the biggest bottom-line benefits—higher sales yields and lower costs of customer acquisitions.

ORC TeleScience synthesizes ORC International's core competencies in market research with the latest teleservices technologies, creating a powerful capability that is redefining the industry.

ORC TELESCIENCE

We offer a full range of teleservices capabilities. Clients benefit from our winning combination of state-of-the-art technology, experienced professionals and strong results-oriented focus. Our goal is to increase sales and reduce costs for our clients.

At the center of ORC TeleScience is the practical application of analytical methodologies based on sophisticated modeling technology, including generalized linear modeling, neural networks and genetic algorithms. These techniques enable ORC TeleScience clients to better understand the customer's purchase decisions, optimize targeting of markets and customers, quantify buyer behavior, provide feedback from customers for "continuous loop" marketing applications and sell products and services.

INVESTORS PRESS AT A GLANCE

PUBLICATIONS · VISIONARY ROUNDTABLES · ACTIONABLE SALES LEADS

Creative Firm   **Silver Communications Inc.**
New York, New York
Client   *Investors Press*

The same weight of white matte paper was used for both cover and text pages of this 8-1/2" x 11" brochure.

1997 INVESTMENT MANAGEMENT BOOK SERIES

The *1997 Investment Management Book Series is written specifically for two audiences: all corporate, public and Taft-Hartley plan sponsors and senior investment officers at foundations and endowments with more than $50 million in tax-exempt assets, and Treasury officials, senior human resource and employee benefits managers of DC plans with more than $10 million in tax-exempt assets. The Small Plan Series serves the burgeoning $1 to $10 million DC market.*

Each book examines issues of compelling concern to these investment professionals in chapters contributed by leading plan sponsors and trustees who candidly share the lessons of their knowledge and experience. Using this unique peer-to-peer dialogue, each book emphasizes practical "how-to" solutions to current problems that help readers improve their professional and investment performance and fulfill their fiduciary responsibilities.

The **Small Plan Edition of Helping Employees Achieve Retirement Security** by Ted Benna, the father of the 401(k), is written specifically for companies with up to $10 million in DC assets or those that are considering or establishing a new savings retirement plan. This updated Guide educates, informs and empowers plan sponsors at small companies who need concise, easy-to-understand information that will help their employees plan for a more secure retirement.

The result of thorough and comprehensive research, this valuable Guide explains 401(k)s in clear, actionable language, answers the most frequently asked 401(k) questions, includes important new information about recent legislation and the new SIMPLE plans and emphasizes why employees should save as much as they can, as early as they can.

Publication: March September

As employees assume greater responsibility for their financial futures, everyone agrees they must be competent financial managers long before and after they retire. But are they ready to assume this responsibility? Do they have the core money management and financial planning skills they need? How far should employee education go to meet these needs? And what potential liabilities do employers face if employees fall short of their retirement objectives?

Beyond the 401(k): Helping Employees Achieve Total Financial Security highlights five very different company case studies, features special tips from leading financial planners and includes an important analysis of liability issues by industry experts. This cutting-edge book helps plan sponsors help employees become better financial managers today, avoid shortfalls tomorrow and maintain financial security well into their retirement years.

Publication: April

As the global marketplace becomes more integrated, experts question the continued diversification benefits of global investing. **How To Identify and Manage Risk In Global Markets** examines the principles driving basic global asset allocation decisions, the advantages and disadvantages of a global approach and the risks involved in various strategies. Readers learn how plan sponsors, investment managers and trustees can communicate with one another more clearly, define organizational structure and responsibilities, develop appropriate checks and balances and evaluate supervisory issues. Managing the hidden risks of benchmarks and knowing how to handle currency risk are among the many risk management tools this book examines and explains.

Publication: May

1997 INVESTMENT MANAGEMENT BOOK SERIES

Besieged by a confusing jumble of products and services that compete for their attention, Treasury officials and HR and EB professionals need impartial guidance on how to deliver top-notch communications, education and superior service. The **DC Plan Sponsor's Handbook: How to Choose, Evaluate and Monitor Providers & Consultants** gives plan sponsors a checklist of questions they should ask to identify their plan's needs. It guides them as they select and monitor those strategic partners and providers who can best help them help their employees plan and prepare for a secure retirement. This important book shows plan sponsors how to build solid partnerships and become more informed buyers and users of pension services.

Publication: September

The **International Pensions Compendium** shares the unique knowledge of U.S. plan sponsors and investment managers with their peers and other institutional investors overseas. The **Compendium** features current, cutting-edge thinking shared by a diverse group of distinguished U.S. plan sponsors who have written chapters in recent IP books. As plan sponsors in other countries re-engineer their pension plans and move toward self-directed defined contribution plans, the range of topics covered in these selected chapters—with a special introduction by RogersCasey and BARRA explaining the significance of the text to the non-U.S. reader—will be a "must read" for overseas plan sponsors.

Publication: October

Communication between plan sponsors, trustees and investment boards can be difficult: too often, there is little shared knowledge or vision. Plan sponsors often avoid innovative solutions, while their partners in pension management frequently rubber-stamp familiar strategies. With trillions of retiree dollars at stake, all plan fiduciaries must learn to speak a common language as they boost plan performance and fulfill their responsibilities to plan participants. **How Plan Sponsors Boost Fiduciary Performance: Speaking A Common Language** teaches readers how various plans have promoted greater fiduciary accountability. It is a thought-provoking book that breaks new ground in helping plan sponsors manage and alleviate the personal career risk they face by implementing cutting-edge investment programs.

Publication: November

The lion's share of working Americans are employed by small to mid-sized companies. As a sequel to the Small Plan Edition of **Helping Employees Achieve Retirement Security**, the **401(k) Plan Sponsor's Compendium** gives small company plan sponsors, many without full-time human resource personnel, important information to help them in their day-to-day plan management. For financial professionals, often forced to wear many hats at small and mid-sized companies, relevant chapters from IP books, enlivened by **Smart Pills** and **Tips From The Trenches**, provide rewarding reading.

Publication: December

Creative Firm   **Mike Salisbury Communications**
Torrance, California
Client   *Rage Magazine*

Brochure measures 9" x
12" and is printed on
Chromecoat.

IS YOUR INTRANET
THIS STRONG, RELIABLE
& FLEXIBLE?

◆Sun

Creative Firm   **Cahan & Associates**
San Francisco,
California
Client   *Sun Microsystems*

Cover and text pages are printed
on the same glossy white stock.
Cover includes a rubber flap which
encourages viewer interaction.
Back inside cover has a pocket to
house other information, and die
cuts to hold a business card.
Brochure is 9" x 12".

IS YOUR INTRANET
THIS STRONG, RELIABLE
& FLEXIBLE?

IT BETTER BE.

◆Sun

182

RAYTHEON & SUN: BLUE SKIES

Raytheon's Electronic Systems has been selected for the new billion-dollar contract to build the Standard Terminal Automation Replacement System (STARS) for the Federal Aviation Administration (FAA) and Department of Defense (DoD). The STARS system will modernize and upgrade 570 Terminal Automation and Tower Systems for the FAA and DoD — providing the critical features and tools needed to allow control and safe separation of aircraft in the airspace around airports and terminals.

Raytheon chose Sun because of its expertise and commitment to providing an open architecture that the FAA can count on now and in the future.

"One of the most important aspects of STARS is that we build it on an open computing foundation," said Jim Burkley, Raytheon Marketing Manager for Transportation Systems. Sun products also provided the best fit for the FAA's mandate to replace key system components with commercial off-the-shelf solutions that are open and easy to upgrade.

Sun's proven quality and adherence to open standards translate directly into benefits for Raytheon as a user and as a contractor to the FAA and Department of Defense. "We and our customers may want to make changes someday, so openness and the ability to change as your business changes are important. You know Sun's going to be around a long time and their stable, industrial-strength products and open architecture assures we'll always be able to get the most current technology from them," Burkley said.

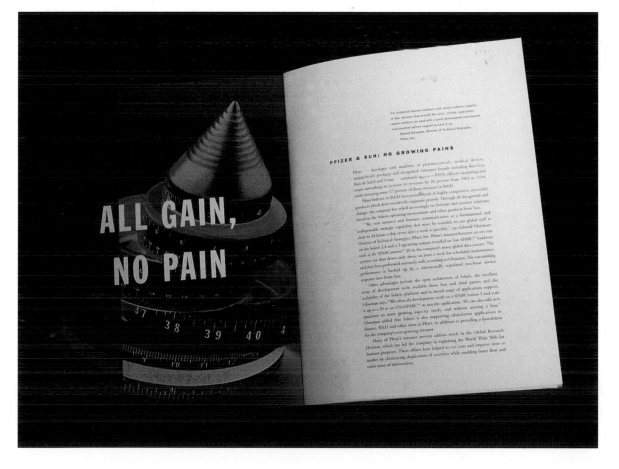

PFIZER & SUN: NO GROWING PAINS

Pfizer — developer and marketer of pharmaceuticals, medical devices, animal-health products and recognized consumer brands including Ben-Gay, Bain de Soleil and Visine — combined aggressive R&D, effective marketing and smart networking to increase its revenues by 26 percent from 1993 to 1994, while investing some 17 percent of those revenues in R&D.

Pfizer believes its R&D investment depends on highly competitive, successful products which drive new levels of corporate growth. Through all this growth and change, the company has relied increasingly on Internet and intranet solutions based on the Solaris operating environment and other products from Sun.

"We view intranet and Internet communications as a fundamental and indispensable strategic capability that must be available to our global staff as close to 24 hours a day, seven days a week as possible," says Edward Glassman, Director of Technical Strategies, Pfizer, Inc. Pfizer's intranet/Internet servers run on the Solaris 2.4 and 2.5 operating systems installed on Sun SPARC™ hardware such as the SPARCstation™ 20 in the company's many global data centers. The systems are that down only about an hour a week for scheduled maintenance, and they have performed extremely well, according to Glassman. The outstanding performance is backed up by a contractually stipulated two-hour service response time from Sun.

Other advantages include the open architecture of Solaris, the excellent array of development tools available from Sun and third parties and the scalability of the Solaris platform and its broad range of applications support. Glassman says, "We often do development work on a SPARCstation 5 and scale it up to a 20 or an UltraSPARC™ to run the application. We can also add new machines to meet growing capacity needs, and without missing a beat." Glassman added that Solaris is also supporting client/server applications in finance, R&D and other areas at Pfizer, in addition to providing a foundation for the company's ever-growing intranet.

Many of Pfizer's intranet services address needs in the Global Research Division, which has led the company in exploiting the World Wide Web for business purposes. These efforts have helped to cut costs and improve time to market by eliminating duplication of activities while enabling faster flow and easier reuse of information.

INDEX